"YOU can't make me"

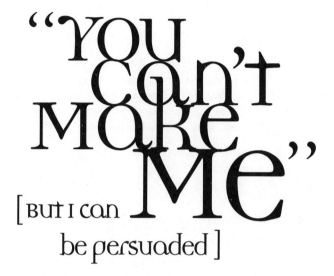

"You can't make me"

[But I can be persuaded]

cynthia ulrich tobias

WATERBROOK
PRESS

YOU CAN'T MAKE ME (BUT I CAN BE PERSUADED)
PUBLISHED BY WATERBROOK PRESS
5446 North Academy Boulevard, Suite 200
Colorado Springs, Colorado 80918
A division of Random House, Inc.

Unless otherwise noted, all Scripture quotations in this publication are from
The Message. Copyright © by Eugene H. Peterson 1993, 1994, 1995. Used by
permission of NavPress Publishing Group. Also cited, the *New American
Standard Bible®* (NASB). © Copyright The Lockman Foundation 1960, 1962,
1963, 1968, 1971, 1972, 1973, 1975, 1977. Used by permission.

Details in some anecdotes and stories have been changed to protect
the identities of the persons involved.

ISBN 1-57856-193-0

Tobias, Cynthia Ulrich, 1953–
      You can't make me, but I can be persuaded… / Cynthia Ulrich
Tobias.—1st ed.
            p.   cm.
      ISBN 1-57856-193-0 (hbk.)
      1. Problem children—Behavior modification—United States. 2. Problem
children—United States—Family relationships. 3. Problem children—
United States—Conduct of life. 4. Child psychology—United States.
5. Individuality in children—United States. 6. Discipline in children—
United States. I. Title.
HQ773.T63   1999
649'.64—dc21   99-20655
                                                                    CIP

Printed in the United States of America
1999—First Edition

10   9   8   7   6   5   4   3

To my strong-willed dad,
R O B E R T   U L R I C H
who has consistently shown me how to use
my strong-willed nature in a way
that brings honor and glory to God.

And to my very patient, compliant mother,
M I N N I E   U L R I C H
who has never quit praying for both of us!

CONTENTS

ACKNOWLEDGMENTS

I would like to gratefully acknowledge the hundreds of Strong-Willed Children (of all ages) who have shared their stories and insights with me. On behalf of all of us, I ask that you read this book with an open mind and a loving heart.

Now here's a surprise:
The master praised the crooked manager!
And why? Because he knew how to look after himself.
Streetwise people are smarter in this regard
than law-abiding citizens. They are on constant alert,
looking for angles, surviving by their wits.
I want you to be smart in the same way—
but for what is right—
using every adversity to stimulate you
to creative survival, to concentrate your attention
on the bare essentials, so you'll live, really live,
and not complacently just get by on good behavior.

Luke 16:8-9

CHAPTER ONE

Who Is the Strong-Willed Child?

Richard loved football, but he didn't care much for studying. By his junior year in high school, his grades were so poor that his diploma was in jeopardy. His parents, it seemed, had tried everything—threats, bribes, promises—to no avail. In desperation, Richard's father issued an ultimatum: "Richard, if you don't get those grades up immediately, you can't play football." And this boy who loved football as much as life itself squared his shoulders, faced his dad, and quietly said, "Then forget football." And everyone lost. Richard lost what he cared about most, and his parents lost what they believed was their only leverage.

She was such an adorable little girl. "Angela!" Her mother sounded exasperated. "Angela, I said get over here *right this minute!*" Standing in the aisle of the department store, I watched the face of this beautiful five-year-old suddenly darken into an angry scowl. "No!" she cried. "I want to go see the toys *now!*" Her mother looked exhausted as she grabbed Angela's hand and began to drag her screaming daughter through the store. As they passed me, I saw the mother's eyes roll upward as she muttered, "Just another ordinary day."

If you are the parent of a strong-willed child (SWC), you don't have any trouble relating to Richard's father or Angela's mother. You've fought hundreds of battles like this with your own child— probably before he or she even turned two years old. You know how frustrating it can be to see your bright, loving, creative offspring instantly turn into a stubborn, immovable force. What did you do to deserve such defiance? How could your wonderful kid have turned into such a monster?

Although much has been written about this "difficult child," Dr. James Dobson, who first introduced us to the term *strong-willed child,* wrote several years ago that he had yet to find "a text for parents or teachers that acknowledges the struggle—the exhausting confrontation of wills—which most parents and teachers experience regularly with their children."[1] Even so, frustrated parents around the world are searching for ways to discipline and direct their stubborn-willed children without breaking their children's seemingly indomitable spirits. In fact, Dr. Dobson writes in his book *The Strong-Willed Child:* "It is my firm conviction that the strong-willed child usually possesses more creative potential and strength of character than his compliant siblings, provided his parents can help him channel his impulses and gain control of his rampaging will."[2]

STRONG-WILLED OR SIMPLY DIFFERENT FROM YOU?

Do you have one of these wild and wonderful children?

How do you know whether you truly have an inherently strong-willed child (SWC) or a child who is temporarily exhibiting defiant behavior? Every individual comes into this world with a wonderfully complex and unique set of traits, characteristics, and temperaments. Research has also shown that we are pre-wired with certain tendencies when it comes to taking in and making sense of information. These preferences, or learning styles, determine how we learn, how we decide what's important, and how we communicate with the rest of the world. These learning styles also play an important part in the parenting process, since we parents often believe our children should do things our way. After all, we are living proof that our way works!

We often overlook, however, that our children have their own views of the world, and we may wear ourselves out trying to change their basic nature as we try to get them to do things that make sense to us. Parents rarely deliberately set out to frustrate their children. Believe it or not, children don't usually try to intentionally annoy their parents either. But when two opposing styles meet, something has to give.

Several months ago on a flight to Orlando, Florida, I sat next to a frustrated parent. Bob is a former fighter pilot for the United States Air Force. He now serves as an instructor as he prepares to retire early. I learned quickly that he has five kids and that two of them are driving him crazy. We laughed good-naturedly, and I began to tell him some of the principles I cover in my book *The Way They Learn*. As we talked about the different learning styles, he was intrigued. "This is beginning to make sense," he claimed. He leaned closer and told me why he was so frustrated with two of his beloved children. "How tough can it be," he asked, "to remember to make a little check mark in a little box on the chart posted on the refrigerator?" Before I could reply, he continued.

"And don't those kids realize that you don't brush your teeth before you put on your pajamas? You put on your pajamas first, then you brush your teeth."

I grinned at him. "Bob, how do you eat M&M's?"

He replied without hesitation. "Oh, I always eat the primary colors first." He looked puzzled. "Why? How do you eat them?"

"Well, I just sort of pour them in my hand and pop them in my mouth."

"Oh no! Don't you realize that the Mars Candy Company has no specific formula for how many of each color go in each individual bag? You can't just consume them *randomly* before you know what you've got!"

I laughed. In jest I said, "Bob, you are a sick man!"

He joined my laughter but suddenly looked thoughtful. "You know, I always just thought my children were being disobedient if they didn't do everything my way. I've already figured out what works best and what methods are most efficient. I assumed that if they do it any other way it's just pure and simple insubordination!"

Bob and I spent the next few hours discovering and celebrating the differences between him and his wife and between him and each of their children. He was delighted to read through the learning styles charts and checklists, and he seemed relieved to learn some ways to motivate and inspire his own SWCs.

You may be convinced that every one of your children could qualify as strong-willed, and yet you may also be surprised to discover that, in many cases, you just have a child who simply makes sense of the world in a unique way. For example, if you tend to be analytic, like Bob, you automatically break information and situations down into component parts, focusing on and remembering specific details. But if you have a child who is the opposite—global—he or she is better at grasping big pictures and getting an overall sense of the situation. While you are demanding that your child pay attention to what you're saying, he may still be struggling to figure out what's so important in the first place. (For more information about these different learning-style combinations, be sure to read my book *The Way They Learn*.)

HOW STRONG-WILLED ARE YOU OR YOUR CHILD?

A strong will, of course, can come in all learning styles. In over a decade of teaching and working with learning styles full-time, however, I have found that SWCs, whether children or adults, have several characteristics in common. Take a few minutes to read the following checklist and mark all the items that describe you personally. Then go through the list again for each of your children and measure the degree of strong will each child appears to possess.

HOW STRONG-WILLED ARE YOU?

Checking Your SWC Quotient

Mark only those statements that are true almost 100% of the time:

The Strong-Willed Child (SWC)...

____ almost never accepts words like "impossible" or phrases like "it can't be done."

____ can move with lightning speed from being a warm, loving presence to being a cold, immovable force.

____ may argue the point into the ground, sometimes just to see how far into the ground the point will go.

____ when bored, has been known to create a crisis rather than have a day go by without incident.

____ considers rules to be more like guidelines (i.e., "As long as I'm abiding by the 'spirit of the law,' why are you being so picky?").

____ shows great creativity and resourcefulness—seems to always find a way to accomplish a goal.

____ can turn what seems to be the smallest issue into a grand crusade or a raging controversy.

____ doesn't do things just because "you're supposed to"—it needs to matter personally.

____ refuses to obey unconditionally—seems to always have a few terms of negotiation before complying.

____ is not afraid to try the unknown—to conquer the unfamiliar (although each SWC chooses his or her own risks, they all seem to possess the confidence to try new things).

____ can take what was meant to be the simplest request and interpret it as an offensive ultimatum.

____ may not actually apologize but almost always makes things right.

Your Score: How Much Strong Will Do You Have?

  0–3   You've got it, but you don't use it much.

  4–7   You use it when you need to, but not on a daily basis.

  8–10 You've got a very healthy dose of it, but you can back off when you want to.

  11–12 You don't leave home without it—and it's almost impossible to not use it.

KEEP A POSITIVE FOCUS

Being strong-willed does not have to be a negative trait! I often remind parents of SWCs that their children may change the world—after all, it's not likely that the world is going to change them! Your SWC may be God's instrument for making the world a better place. It is a great gift to have a child with firm convictions, a high spirit, and a sense of adventure. Think about some of the great leaders and innovators in our past—Thomas Jefferson, Marie Curie, Albert Einstein, Joan of Arc, Thomas Edison, and others. Each of these people held up under adversity, stood up for his or her convictions, and persisted against all odds. They refused to believe their dreams were impossible.

Of course, some SWCs may travel a rocky road on the way to their success, and parents will certainly have an abundance of opportunities to develop patience and creative discipline techniques. Franklin Graham, an SWC and the older son of evangelist Billy Graham, gives many wonderful examples of this in his autobiography, *Rebel with a Cause*. One of my favorites is the story he tells about his mother's tactic to cure him of his smoking habit.

My habit of finding cigarette butts and smoking them got so bad that when Floyd Roberts, our caretaker, came up to the house one evening to see how everything was, Mama asked to borrow the pack of cigarettes he was carrying in his pocket.

"I'm going to teach Franklin a lesson," she told Floyd.

She brought me into the kitchen and sat me down in front of the fireplace. *What is she up to?* I wondered.

She opened the pack, pulled out a cigarette, and handed it to me. "Now light it and smoke it—and be sure to inhale!" Mama wanted me to get sick, thinking that if I threw up I would never want to touch a cigarette again.

I couldn't believe Mama was actually giving me permission to smoke! I remembered Daddy telling me how his daddy whipped the taste right out of his mouth when he was a boy after Granddaddy caught him smoking—and it had worked! So I was surprised that Mama was actually letting me smoke with her blessing. This was great.

"Sure," I said, and lit the first cigarette and inhaled deeply.

Mama watched as I puffed, her face expressionless. "Keep smoking," she said.

I did. When I finished the second one, my face turned as green as a cow's cud. I ran into the bathroom and threw up. I washed my face and headed back to the kitchen for more. I picked up the third cigarette, and with a cocky grin, struck the match and went at it again. Within minutes, I raced back to the bathroom to puke again. I wasn't easily deterred.

By the time I had finished all twenty, I must have vomited five or six times. I felt horrible. Every time I got sick, I'm sure Mama thought her approach was working, but it gave me great satisfaction not to give in. That wasn't the result Mama wanted.

I wasn't sure my stomach would ever stop churning. But if there had been another pack of cigarettes, I probably would have smoked them too!

Mama didn't give up trying to make me quit smoking, but she never used that tactic again.[3]

Every SWC I know who has read this story identifies with Franklin's determination. Today, the former prodigal is assuming his father's place as the head of the Billy Graham Evangelistic Association, one of the most influential Christian organizations this world has ever known. His strong will is sure to be an asset as he faces this challenge.

IT TAKES ONE TO KNOW ONE!

I have talked to thousands of SWCs over the past several years, including hundreds of prodigal sons and daughters, and they have given me a wealth of information to share with you. Their answers are consistent, and their insights are valuable.

I have also lived my life seeing firsthand how the mind of the SWC works—from the inside out. I was never what you would call a rebellious or defiant child. I grew up the daughter of a conservative, evangelical preacher, and I never rebelled against my dad or caused him to feel ashamed of me. I was not a particularly loud or obnoxious child. I never talked back to a teacher. In fact, you couldn't have traced half the trouble I caused back to me! Outwardly, I was quiet and compliant and basically easy to get along with.

But whenever I am backed into a corner and told "Do it…or else," I simply "else." I may not be confrontational or loud, but I know there is nothing I really have to do—except die, which I am willing to do. And since I am willing to die and you're not, I win. (Okay, I'm dead, but I win.) As you can imagine, this mind-set has always presented a unique challenge to my parents and others in authority over me.

My mother tells me that as early as eighteen months I had already figured out no one could really *make* me do anything. She tried to insist I eat all the food that was placed before me. As soon as I figured out she was going to have me sit there until the food was gone, I simply dumped the contents of the bowl on top of my head. It became a contest each meal to see if Mom could figure out which bite was my last one before the bowl was dumped and she had a mess to clean up. It didn't take long for her to decide the battle wasn't worth it!

My sister came along five years after I did, and she was nothing like me. Since it took my parents that long to work up the courage to have another child, I think they were relieved to find Sandee so compliant and pleasant natured. As the oldest, I used my position and strong-willed nature to both delight and traumatize my sister. I was definitely in charge, and Sandee followed my lead. Sometimes the bully, often the dictator or even the encourager, I enjoyed having my sister recognize and appreciate my strengths.

Although my mother was convinced we would never be able to do anything but fight with each other, as adults Sandee and I are very close and enjoy a wonderful relationship. People often ask her if she grew up resenting me because I was such an SWC. She sweetly smiles and claims it was actually a blessing. "You see," she explains, "I loved it. Since Cindy was always the one with the dangerous or adventurous ideas, I was never the one to get in trouble. I would just say it wasn't my idea, wasn't my fault—and Mom knew I was telling the truth."

Even though I'm an SWC myself, I believe my best credentials for speaking out on behalf of all SWCs is that I am the parent of a strong-willed son. (My mother denies she prayed this would happen so I would know what it was like!) My son Michael is so typical of the SWC. At one moment he is loving and thoughtful; at the next he is relentlessly terrorizing his brother or mouthing off to his father.

I am forced to live what I teach every day. I am not giving you advice from a quiet corner. I am in the trenches with you. I know firsthand that having an SWC can be both the best and worst thing that can happen to you. Mike is strong and intelligent and determined. He can ruthlessly drive himself to master a task or achieve a goal. And yet the strength of his will is often at its worst when obstacles stand in the way of his plans or when his twin brother, Robert, is not his normally compliant self. Mike can quickly change from a focused, analytic child to a frustrated, impatient kid, loudly demanding his way. At times like this I hear him screaming at his brother.

"You're *fired*, Robert! You're not my *brother* anymore!" Of course, if Robert calls his bluff and walks away, Mike is quick to call him back—immediately suggesting at least a slight compromise.

If any of this sounds familiar, you've come to the right place! I'm about to offer you more hope and encouragement about your relationship with your SWC than you may have thought possible. I know we SWCs can drive you crazy. We know how to push the buttons that reduce you to rage in a matter of seconds. We seem to constantly choose to do things the hard way. School and other traditional functions may leave us bored, frustrated, and restless.

But if you are the parent of an SWC, you have been given the opportunity to love, nurture, and guide an individual who has great potential. Why not direct that wonderful and mysterious energy into the right channels, and use that marvelous determination to achieve positive results? True, you will be stretched and challenged beyond what you thought were your limits. But ultimately you can be rewarded with an SWC who loves God, who loves you, and who leaves your home with the ability to be a successful adult.

This book can place in your hands a priceless treasure—the gift of understanding your SWC. I hope to give you a glimpse into the mind of an SWC so you can begin to see how it works. I want to offer you practical strategies for how to motivate and inspire your SWC rather than to simply engage in power struggles and pointless battles. I will offer guidelines to help you determine whether you need to do something drastic. What you are about to read and think about can heal your relationship with your SWC, bring peace to an argumentative family, and help you discover some wonderful things about yourself in the process.

Most of all, I hope this book shows you that instead of simply becoming exasperated and irritated with your SWC, you can honor and value what he or she does best while still holding every individual accountable for moral and spiritual values.

Hang on, and keep an open mind!

Real wisdom, God's wisdom,
begins with a holy life and is characterized by
getting along with others.... You can develop a healthy,
robust community that lives right with God
and enjoy its results
only if you do the hard work
of getting along with each other,
treating each other with dignity and honor.

James 3:17-18

CHAPTER TWO

How Do I Build a Positive Relationship with My Strong-Willed Child?

I just can't believe he would do this to us! We raised him to be a good boy—we've always trusted him, and now *this!*" The camera panned from the distraught mother to her sullen thirteen-year-old son, the object of her anger and disappointment.

They appeared on a morning network news and talk show that I happened to be watching from my hotel room. Apparently the show's week had been devoted to stories about kids on drugs, exposing problems and offering solutions. This particular morning the show touted at-home drug tests and showcased a teenage boy who had been caught doing drugs, and his parents, who were determined he would not get away with it.

The frightened and angry mother told the reporter how terrible the situation had been for her, and she quickly outlined the plan she and her husband had launched to turn their son around. Their tough-love contract was inflexible, and an at-home drug test would be ready at a moment's notice. Although the camera focused on the mom's face, I watched her son in the background. As I studied his face, I couldn't help thinking he knew he was in trouble. He knew he had made a mistake. He knew he would have to pay some stiff penalties. What I *don't* think he knew, however, was that his parents still loved him. You see, his mom didn't say: "We almost lost this boy, and he is so important to us. He is such a valuable part of our family, and we love him so much that we'll do anything we have to in order to bring him back. If it takes tough love, drug tests, even a lockdown or rehabilitation program, we'll do whatever it takes because we love him and we want him back."

But she didn't say that, and her son slouched in the background with a posture and attitude somewhere between dejection and defiance. As the reporter wrapped up the segment, he turned the camera on the boy.

"Son," he said, "tell me—what do *you* think of all this?" The teenager looked directly and intensely into the camera and said, "I can't wait to leave home."

As the shot faded, I almost cried. Did these parents really think it was worth it? By taking this heavy-handed approach, they had lost their son. Instead of bringing him back, they were driving him farther away. I don't believe they meant to do that. I think they honestly thought they were doing the best they could under the circumstances. But they overlooked a vital part of the solution: They had not fostered the kind of relationship with their son that he wanted to preserve.

Even when he *wasn't* annoying and disobeying them, did they still scold him? Had this boy's parents invested the time and effort it takes to let him know they really enjoyed having him around? When they taught him to do the right things, had they also noticed and appreciated the times he chose to follow their lead? If they had taken time to build the kind of relationship their son would want to hang on to, their words of rebuke and harsh calls for change might have been effective. But if they had spent the last few years yelling at him more often than they spoke kindly to him, if they always seemed to notice what went wrong and simply said nothing when things went right, their son may have felt he essentially had nothing to lose. If his parents were going to yell and be mad at him no matter what, why should he even try?

Throughout every book or article I've written, I've talked about some basic parenting principles that apply to every parent-child relationship. When it comes to relating to the SWC, these principles take on even more significance, since almost everything in the relationship—both positive and negative—tends to be more extreme.

One of these fundamental principles is this:

CONSISTENTLY SHOW YOUR CHILD NOT ONLY LOVE, BUT ALSO VALUE AND RESPECT

Every SWC I've known (including me) has told me essentially the same thing: If a person doesn't care *about* me, I don't care what he or she does *to* me. I put it simply in my book *Every Child Can Succeed*:

> The quality of the relationship you have with each child will determine the effectiveness of the techniques you use. If you have cultivated a loving and healthy relationship with each of your children, they will care very much about preserving it. If there is no benefit in keeping the parental relationship intact, your efforts to discipline and motivate may have little or no effect.

Even the child with the strongest will responds more to love and genuine kindness than to creative or flashy methods and approaches.[1]

I have had many angry and frustrated parents assert that their SWC "has to learn to get along with the world." I gently remind them that jails are full of people who didn't have to get along with the world. Why not motivate your SWC to *want* to get along with the world in the first place? Then, if he or she has a strong and positive relationship with you, you'll be the one your child turns to for advice on how to do it.

This principle can be challenging to the parent of an SWC because we SWCs don't make it easy for you to love us. You say, "I'll love you no matter what." And some of us say, "Really? How about this? Will you love me now? How about *this*?" Sometimes, as we experiment or make mistakes or even do outrageous things, we find out you don't love us no matter what. You love us *if* we do things your way and *if* we follow your rules. We don't expect you to let us get by with bad behavior, but we count on the fact that our relationship with you will stay intact no matter what.

I remember a particularly difficult day with my then-two-year-old SWC. I was sure he had spent the day irritating me on purpose. Just when I reached the end of my patience, he led me into the playroom. While I stood there, he crawled inside the empty toy cabinet and began to close the door. He leaned toward me and said loudly, "Go away!" Then he slammed the door. Although I secretly wanted to escape, I remained there. In a moment, the door flew open and there was a startled yet pleased expression on his face. "You didn't go away!" he declared. Then he gave me a more serious look. *"Go away!"*

As we played the go-away-you-didn't-go-away game, I thought about how many SWCs, especially adolescents, tell their parents things like: "I hate you! Go away! Get out of my life! I never want to see you again!" Then they slam the door. Inside, they secretly, desperately hope you won't go away. They open the door, and you're still there. "I *told* you to go away! I *mean* it! I hate you! Leave me alone!" And they slam the door even harder. They wonder, *Did that do it? Did I really drive them away this time?*

Almost all of the SWCs I've talked to admit they often feel driven to find out whether their parents' love is truly unconditional. SWCs need to know there is nothing they can do that would actually make you stop loving them. They know there is a price to pay for making a wrong decision, but they have to know that losing your love will not be part of the cost. When SWCs feel secure in your love, you may be surprised at how seldom they test it.

Another fundamental parenting principle is to:

CHOOSE YOUR BATTLES CAREFULLY—MOST AREN'T WORTH SACRIFICING THE RELATIONSHIP

When I was growing up, my dad was the ultimate authority in our house. My SWC nature did not question him when he laid down the law. But you see, Dad intuitively knew a parenting technique that is critical for dealing with the SWC. If he said "Cindy! Sit down. *Now!*" I just sat. I didn't question or argue. I knew my dad wouldn't talk to me like that unless it was essential that I obey. If he *had* talked to me like that all the time, I would have tuned him out and not done *anything* he asked. Parents take note: If you use the same angry tone of voice for everything (*"You get upstairs to bed!" "You eat the rest of that dinner!" "You get dressed right now!"*), you'll soon find your SWCs arguing with you about everything.

It's difficult to maintain a positive and loving relationship with your SWC if the two of you are constantly battling for control. Parents often find themselves raising their voices and losing their tempers. Before they realize it, most of the communication between them and their SWC consists of harsh words and angry directives. If this is the case in your home, you can change the pattern. In order to avoid a confrontation when you want your child to obey you, ask yourself these important questions: Is it worth it? Is this battle worth fighting? Will this improve the quality of our relationship?

In our home there are certain nonnegotiable issues: (1) physical safety, e.g., we don't walk in front of moving cars or ride without seat belts, and (2) moral and spiritual values, e.g., we don't lie or hurt others. Beyond those, we try to let our SWC negotiate to a certain extent.

One cold winter morning when my son Michael was only four, he started to walk out the door without his sweater. Because I know how an SWC's mind works, I offered him an option: "Mike, do you want to wear your red sweater or your blue sweater?" Quick as a flash, he turned to me and replied, "I don't want to wear a sweater." I had to fight my natural response, which was to tell him he certainly *was* going to wear a sweater and he had better decide which one or I was going to decide for him. But I knew I couldn't *make* him wear anything. Would this battle be worth ruining our morning together?

Swallowing my frustration, I asked him another question. "Mike, what do you want to wear to keep warm?" He paused for a moment and shrugged before he replied. "I want to wear Daddy's sweater," he stated matter-of-factly. Again I fought my desire to tell him that was totally absurd and to put on his own sweater. I asked Daddy if Mike could wear one of his sweaters, and he agreed. My four-year-old SWC was almost lost inside of it. He looked ridiculous, and I wanted to attach a sign to his back that stated "My mother didn't dress me!" Instead, I tucked one of Mike's sweaters under my arm and we went on with our day. It took less than fifteen minutes for Mike to grow weary of struggling with the oversize sweater. Resisting the urge to say "I told you so," I casually asked him if he would like to have his own sweater on instead of Daddy's. Without hesitating, he nodded, took off the bulky garment, and put on his own. Just like that. No big deal.

Next time you want your SWC to do something (and you want to avoid a power struggle), first decide whether the battle is worth it. The process won't be easy, and it may take a lot of practice before you and your SWC can distinguish negotiable issues from nonnegotiable ones. But the effort can make a tremendous difference in your relationship.

A few years ago, I spoke to a group of parents at a conservative private school. Afterward, one mother waited quite awhile for her turn to talk to me. She was agitated and upset.

"Listen," she said, "I have a strong-willed daughter. I admit I have been very strict, and I am at times inflexible. But I've kept my thumb on my daughter, and she knows who's boss around our house." She paused and pointed to the doorway of the gymnasium. Standing there was a sullen, angry-looking twelve-year-old, smacking her gum and impatiently tapping her foot. Her mom turned back to me, and her eyes brimmed with tears.

"That's my daughter. She hates me. She'd sell me down the river for a nickel. Do you have anything that would get her to love me again?"

Here was a mom who had demanded unquestioned obedience, who had ruled with an iron hand. Had she forced her daughter to obey? Yes, to a certain extent. But this mother did not realize until that day what price she had paid for her daughter's compliance. Her adolescent girl couldn't wait to leave home, couldn't wait to turn from everything her mother held dear. Their relationship was broken. Was that kind of obedience worth it?

BUT WHAT IF THE PARENTS DON'T AGREE?

Some of you reading this are nodding your heads, agreeing with me. But you're thinking about your spouse, who may not understand this point at all. It's common for one parent to appear to be more tolerant and understanding of an SWC than the other, even though both parents care very much about their child. What about such families, in which an SWC has a close relationship with one parent but not the other? What about single parents who struggle to keep their children's lives from falling apart? And what about blended families, who face uniquely challenging relationships? No matter how trying your circumstances, it's possible to establish and maintain a strong positive relationship with your SWC.

When Your SWC Plays One Parent Against the Other
Although a parent may not consciously play favorites, it's not unusual for a mom or dad to be at odds with a child who won't simply do as he or she is told. It doesn't take long for the SWC to figure out how to play one parent against the other.

Susan has always been close to her father. An SWC himself, her dad tried to allow Susan some flexibility and options and rarely raised his voice or punished her. Susan's mother was reared in the home of a career military officer, and she thought her husband indulged their daughter too often. After all, Mom believed, rank has its privilege, and children should give their parents unquestioned obedience and learn to follow instructions to the letter. Mom considered her husband's tendency to let Susan have so much decision-making input a weakness. She said she loved her daughter too much to let her stray far from the line. Susan's dad argued that he was simply helping Susan learn to be an independent thinker.

Susan hated doing her homework every evening. Appealing to her dad, she often convinced him that the homework could wait so they "could have some fun together." Susan's mom insisted that work should always take priority over play; Susan's dad pointed out that the work would always be there and that their daughter was quickly growing up. Susan came to see her father as the one who let her do the fun things and her mom as the one who held her back. Her relationship with her mother was strained at best.

By the time Susan was a teenager, the conflict between her parents had reached an unbearable level. On the verge of divorce, the parents turned to a wise marriage-and-family counselor. Susan, of course, needed both parents' perspectives and values. She needed to exhibit good behavior and learn self-discipline. She also needed freedom to make her own decisions and to become responsibly independent. The counselor suggested Susan's parents work out agreeable ground rules for rearing Susan.

Although the exercise was late in coming, they both agreed to make the effort. They often asked each other, "What's the point? What are we trying to accomplish with Susan?" Once they defined the goals—physical safety, personal responsibility, etc.—they were able to hold an after-dinner family conference, share their list of goals with Susan, and involve her in deciding upon some of the methods for achieving them.

Curfew, for example, was a big family issue. Susan hated coming in by ten on weekend nights when most of her friends were staying out until midnight. Mom insisted that she trusted Susan, but she wanted Susan to be safe. Dad argued that Susan needed to take responsibility for her own decisions. Both parents agreed, however, that Susan's safety was the first priority. Susan and her parents agreed to a midnight curfew on Fridays and Saturdays, with possible exceptions if she called beforehand and informed them where she was and when she would be home. Dad admitted it was necessary to keep track of his daughter's whereabouts, and Mom agreed to trust her daughter's judgment until she had reason not to.

Although it has taken over a year to see a significant improvement in the relationship between Susan and her mom, the marriage began to recover almost immediately. Over time Susan's mother has learned to communicate her love and respect for her daughter by giving her room to negotiate. Susan's dad has been able to show his daughter that fun can be a part of accountability, and Susan recognizes that although her parents ask her to submit to their authority, they clearly appreciate and respect her.

When You Are a Single Parent with an SWC

Most single parents find themselves in this situation due to death or divorce. As a result their SWCs may feel insecure and even angry, causing them to test their parents' love. Consistently showing love and respect for a child who is angry or confused may be one of the most difficult tasks you have ever undertaken. If it seems you've lost your ability to stay calm and loving when your SWC has figured out what it takes to make you "lose it," this next illustration may help.

"It's not fair! I hate it here! I'm going to go live with my dad!" If Sally had heard that cry once, she had heard it a hundred times from her ten-year-old son, Ryan. For over two years, Ryan had held the threat over her head like emotional blackmail. Today, it was different. *She* was different. Sally took a deep breath and began to put into practice her new parenting approach.

"Ryan, if you go, I will miss you terribly. But I can't make you stay." She heard her voice stay calm, and she wasn't sure who was more surprised, she or Ryan. He looked at her suspiciously.

"You *want* me go live with Dad?" he asked. Sally smiled and shook her head.

"No, of course not. I want you here with me. But you and I both know the rules around here. If there's just no way you can live with them, and if you're determined to go live with your dad, I will not force you to stay."

Ryan frowned. "But your rules are *stupid*. Dad *never* makes me do all this stuff at his house." Sally nodded empathetically.

"I know," she said simply, fighting the urge to make further comment. She stood looking at her son as he watched her face for some sign of anger.

She prayed for the strength to hold her ground with Ryan. He knew the words that could make her crazy. He had always been able to push every hot button she had when it came to arguments. But she was determined to hold on to her fragile relationship with him. She had watched it begin to crumble after the divorce and had felt helpless to keep it from breaking apart completely. Ryan was so good at manipulating, so quick to grab opportunities to play his parents against each other. And Sally had been at the end of her rope with so many things at once—the divorce, the stress of her job, the guilt about what the whole situation was doing to Ryan. She had found herself yelling at him for almost everything. But she knew more now. She was not about to let her son slip away.

Ryan had been waiting for her to react in her usual way, and he was uncertain what to do when she wasn't yelling at him. His resolve seemed to be crumbling. Sally reached over to give him a quick hug.

"Ryan, do you know what I like about you?" she asked. When he shook his head, her heart almost broke. Was it possible he didn't know how much she loved him?

"Sweetheart, I like the way you help me keep this house together when I feel that everything's falling apart. I like how you watch my favorite old TV show with me every night before bed and then let me tuck you in. And I especially like how you stand up for what you believe, even when others may not agree with you. Ryan, you are a wonderful kid, and I am so lucky to have you."

Ryan tried not to smile, but he didn't resist her hug. "Does that mean I don't have to take the trash out after all?" he asked. Sally gave him a playful shove.

"Nice try," she told him. "How about I *help* you, and we'll get it done twice as fast?"

He shrugged and nodded. "I need to call Dad," he said. Sally's heart almost stopped. Ryan nodded again. "I think I'd better tell him I won't be seeing him until this weekend after all."

Being a single parent presents an incredible and exhausting challenge, even when you have a compliant child. Put an SWC into the mix, and it can be a recipe for disaster! But a couple of practical solutions can bring quick relief.

- *Try "trading" SWCs with another single parent for a day.*
  Often a change of perspective can give you a little

breathing room. Also, sometimes dealing with a different SWC can help you be more objective with your own. When you trade back, be sure you and the other parent share some of the things you liked best about each other's SWC. Start out with something similar to this: "One of the things I like most about Josh is..."

- *Ask a parent you admire to be your mentor—preferably someone who has succeeded in raising an SWC of his or her own.* Find someone who would welcome occasional phone calls and give sensitive, nonjudgmental advice. Make it easy for your prospective mentor—don't ask for lengthy answers or request time out of a too-busy schedule. Tell him or her what you propose to do in a particular situation, and get feedback and suggestions. Don't feel self-conscious about asking for help when you're overwhelmed. Most good mentors will be honored that you've asked for their advice.

When You Have a Blended Family and an SWC
It is especially challenging to deal with the SWC in blended families. Not only do you have the task of adjusting to a new spouse, but you might also have to accept and accommodate children

with complex and mysterious learning styles and personality traits that were not in any way inherited from you.

I have spoken to dozens of moms and dads who are struggling to love and understand an SWC who seems determined to undermine the new family structure. One frustrated mother admitted she had reached the point with her twelve-year-old SWC stepson where she simply no longer wanted to spend the energy trying to love him. "I take care of his physical needs," she assured me, "but I just won't let him jerk my emotions around anymore. He thinks I hate him, and I'm so tired of going head to head with him every day that I think I'll just let him see that I'm withdrawing from the whole relationship."

I understand this woman's frustration. She is an SWC herself, and her almost-teenage stepson has figured out the quickest way to drive her into a corner almost every time they speak to each other. He knows how to pit his father against his stepmother, and he uses his biological mother as another piece of ammunition. He gets by with a lot of bad behavior, and she feels powerless to enforce the rules without her husband's full support.

This situation is all too familiar. Discipline, of course, must stay intact. In chapter 5, we will discuss some practical and effective strategies for disciplining the SWC. At no time do I advocate letting the SWC get by with bad behavior. But before any discipline strategies can have the desired effect, a positive relationship must be established between all parties involved. I have dealt with many parents who have reached the end of their ropes with their biological children. It's no wonder that parents struggle when they have to learn to love another person's difficult child. But you simply can't have a healthy family without building and sustaining a loving and respectful relationship with each child. Of course each child needs to respect his or her parents as well, but since we're the grownups, we need to set the example.

When a parent gives up and decides to withdraw from the relationship with a child, devastating results almost always follow. A family cannot survive without unconditional love for one another. That does not mean you must accept whatever behavior your child decides to give you. Instead, it means that you maintain a firm but loving attitude even when you have to take fairly drastic steps to enforce the rules and consequences.

An SWC knows you can't force him to love or accept you. He also knows he doesn't *have* to do what you say. The one thing he does *not* know is whether or not you will really keep loving him no matter what. After all, he's already lost at least one parent. What assurance does he have that you'll stick around for him? It won't be easy, but you can help him develop confidence in you and in his new family situation.

Look for ways you can show him how serious you are about your commitment to the blended family. Even small gestures can mean a lot to a kid who is looking for signs of security. For example:

- *Suggest putting together a time capsule.* Ask all the members of the family to contribute items that will always remind them of this turning point in their lives. Encourage each one to write at least a brief note about how he's feeling, then seal the notes and the items in an envelope. Decide together what date in the future you will open the time capsule.

- *Look for opportunities to talk about your future as a new family.* For example, buy tickets for a show that's months in the future, or post a calendar that tracks a full year's activities.

- *When your SWC (or any of your children) witnesses an argument between you and your new spouse, take time to reassure him the relationship is still strong and loving.* No matter how difficult the adjustments are, your children need to know your love will stay intact. Your respect for each child's unique contributions to the family will build and cement the lifelong relationship.

NEVER GIVE UP!

Some of you reading this may have lost the drive and energy it takes to start over and restore a good relationship with your SWC. What can you do if you have lost the will to go on? What if the whole situation simply seems too overwhelming? I don't believe parents of SWCs can cultivate and maintain these often fragile relationships on our own. We have too many limitations and too much pride and stubbornness within ourselves to deal with a defiant or rebellious child.

Over the many years that I have been an SWC, have raised an SWC, and have worked with parents of SWCs, I have seen only one effective solution for rebuilding and recovering relationships that are so far gone: God, who created us in the first place, can restore love and renew the desire to keep our relationships strong and healthy. On our own, we humans simply don't have the resources to maintain the energy to deal with the daily challenges of loving and living with the SWC.

If you feel that you have exhausted your options—if you have *had* it—and you don't see any way to rebuild your relationship with your SWC, let me offer you the best hope I have found, bar none. Trust the wisdom of the God who created your SWC in the first place. Pray for guidance and wisdom and, most of all, the desire to love your child unconditionally. It takes more strength than you have, but God has an abundant store of mercy and grace, and it is when we reach the end of our own resources that He can do His best. Don't despair if things don't change immediately. Keep praying, and keep working on *your* attitude. Don't give up! With God's help you can do this!

KEY INSIGHTS FROM THE HEART OF AN SWC

- It's the special relationship with you, not how many parenting techniques or strategies you know, that makes the most difference to me.
- Most of the time I am *not* trying to annoy you on purpose. I just want you to appreciate my uniqueness. I want you to see *me* and love me no matter what.
- If you love me and value me, I'll do almost anything for you.

God can do anything, you know—
far more than you could ever imagine
or guess
or request in your wildest dreams!
He does it not by pushing us around
but by working within us,
his Spirit deeply and gently within us.

Ephesians 3:20

CHAPTER THREE

How Do I Motivate My Strong-Willed Child?

Ninth-grader Shannon received her term project assignment almost six weeks before its due date. After an initial burst of enthusiasm about choosing her topic, she set the project aside until the weekend before it was due. By Saturday night, the pressure she felt had spread through the whole family. Her mom was frustrated that Shannon had waited until the last minute to start a project that was supposed to be accomplished over a six-week period. After the flurry of brainstorming and supply gathering, Shannon spread her materials over the dining room table and most of the kitchen counters while she tackled the assignment.

During the next forty-eight hours, Shannon took at least twenty-two study breaks and ten or twelve snack breaks. The family walked around mountains of books and papers and ordered out for pizza. Tempers flared and patience was in short supply, but at 1:00 A.M. on Monday, Shannon completed her project. That morning she left for school, seemingly unaware of the chaos and frustration she left behind as she closed the front door.

David was almost five, and he still wasn't potty trained. His frustrated mother had tried everything. She had promised him coveted toys, threatened to embarrass him in front of his friends, tried to shame him, and experimented with dozens of punishments and rewards. Nothing had worked, and Mom was at the end of her rope. What was it going to take?

Finally she found a pediatrician who seemed sympathetic. "Tell me what to do," she pleaded with the doctor. "I'm ready for anything."

The doctor smiled. "It's too important to you," he said simply. "It matters too much. Just back off and stop making it such an issue."

David's mom was incredulous. "But it *is* an issue! He's almost five years old!"

The doctor shook his head. "It's under his control," he reminded her. "You can't make him do this, and he knows it."

Joanne was a normal twelve-year-old, but her mom had prayed for years that her daughter would become an exception in just one small way—she would learn to keep her bedroom neat and tidy. Since Joanne had weathered several attempts on the part of her mother to accomplish this goal, overall the cause seemed hopeless. Was her daughter destined to be the messiest child on the face of the earth? Would she ever learn to be organized and neat?

A month or so later, Joanne's mom went to school for the parent-teacher conference. Joanne's teacher was full of praise for one of her "very best" students. "Why, even her desk is immaculate and organized!" Joanne's mother couldn't believe they were talking about the same girl, but she looked at her daughter's desk in amazement. Every pencil was sharpened; every piece of paper and every one of the school supplies was lined up and categorized. How could this be? How could Joanne be so fastidious at school and yet be such a slob at home?

Do any of these scenarios sound familiar? Do you ever wonder why it is so difficult to motivate your SWC to achieve the best?

Charlie Brown of the Peanuts cartoon strip once complained, "There's no heavier burden than a great potential!" As a parent, you can see your child's many wonderful possibilities from the beginning, and it's hard not to press him or her firmly in those directions. A child's unwillingness to attempt what you know he or she is capable of can create a tremendous amount of tension between the two of you. Most parents fall into the habit of threatening, bribing, coercing, and yelling. When nothing seems to work, the process just keeps being repeated.

Dr. Dobson described the problem this way:

There is no more ineffective method of leading human beings (of all ages) than the use of irritation and anger. Nevertheless, *most* adults rely primarily on their own emotional response to secure the cooperation of children. One teacher said on a national television program, "I like being a professional educator, but I hate the daily task of teaching. My children are so unruly that I have to stay mad at them all the time just to control the classroom." How utterly frustrating to be required to be mean and angry as part of a routine assignment, year in and year out. Yet many teachers (and parents) know of no other way to lead children. Believe me, it is exhausting and it doesn't work![1]

So what does work? Obviously you can't just let your SWC drift along with no ambition, no drive. And you certainly can't tolerate laziness or bad behavior. The good news is you don't have to.

I believe that the insights SWCs have to share with you in this chapter can make a huge difference when it comes to motivating your own SWC. Before you read them, however, I ask you to set aside your frustration and anger. Put away your determination to have your child do things your way. You will not have to sacrifice accountability, but you may need a new perspective on how to get your SWC to the desired outcome.

If you want to motivate any child, the following parenting principle is helpful, but it's essential if you ever hope to motivate your SWC:

DEFINE THE OUTCOME BY ASKING
"WHAT'S THE POINT?"

I introduced the concept of asking what's the point in chapter 2. In order to help you understand why this is so important, let me show you how the mind of an SWC works. We want to know what the purpose of a task or goal is, mostly so we can decide whether it is worth the effort to achieve it. After all, who established the goal in the first place? Why? Once we understand what the end result is supposed to be, what if we can find a better way to get there? SWCs are not usually trying to irritate you by posing these questions. Instead, we are genuinely attempting to figure out what to think and how to stay in control of our world.

Let's say you decided to hand out a list of household chores to your children. I am the SWC who gets the job of taking out the garbage the day the sanitation truck picks it up. Sounds simple, but right away I protest. "Why do I have to take out the trash?" Your natural response is, "Because that's your job." Uh-oh. Wrong answer. Who decided that was my job? Why didn't I get to pick? I'll bet you're impatient with me already. After all, I'm the child and you're the parent. End of discussion. Or is it? How do you get to the what's-the-point question in this case?

SWCs would rather have compelling problems to solve than have just a list of chores to do. Try soliciting my input regarding the chores. For example, you can say something like this: "We have a problem. The trash truck comes on Tuesday. Your father has an early meeting; I have to get the twins ready for school. Someone has to get the trash out to the curb before the 8:00 A.M. pickup. Any suggestions?"

I may or may not have one right away. It may or may not be a solution that's satisfactory to you. But you're including me in the loop. You're letting me know what you're thinking and why you're about to ask me to do the Tuesday trash pickup. If I tell you I don't want to do it, remind me that my brothers and sisters are sharing in the chores and that everyone needs to be pulling his or her weight. What do I have in mind for dividing the labor? Maybe I can come up with a creative answer you'll like. Maybe I'll just agree to go ahead and do the trash. For me, the important thing is that I'm helping you solve a problem, not just blindly obeying your commands.

Sometimes the solution is as easy as asking a question: "Do you know why I want you to do this?" If you handle this question effectively, you can strengthen your child's ability to think independently. As you work to get your SWC's cooperation, keep reminding yourself to focus on the point of each task. What are you trying to accomplish? Is there another way to do it? Are you challenging your child to think about the possibilities? Are you prepared to let him or her actually try some of those possibilities?

MAKE SURE YOUR SWC IS COMMITTED TO ACHIEVING THE GOAL

Once, in Seattle, Washington, one of my learning-styles graduate professors opened class with an offer to send us all to Cleveland. He said he would give us several options for getting there. We could go by air, by train, by bus, by whatever means we chose. We could even get creative and go by bicycle or hot-air balloon.

He must have known we would think he was crazy. After a few moments, he paused and smiled. Then he made his point. "If you don't *want* to go to Cleveland," he said, "it won't matter how many imaginative and wonderful methods I offer to *get* you there. All the creative teaching or parenting strategies in the world won't help you if you haven't motivated the child to *want* to get where you're going."

It makes sense. In the process of convincing our children to do what we want, we often overlook the fact that they aren't committed to achieving our goals. You can't *make* your child want what you want. What you can do is inspire, motivate, and persuade.

Take the typical battle parents wage with children who refuse to sit at the table and eat the food set before them. They need to eat, right? They can't live on junk food and snacks, right? So you insist they eat what is good for them whether they like it or not. But again, you can't really *make* them eat anything. And your explanation that it's good for them simply isn't convincing. So how can you motivate that distracted, finicky SWC to eat healthy and nutritious foods?

Although every SWC is a little different, most of us respond generally well to requests that we do something we believe will benefit us personally. Add to that our spirit of competition and our low resistance to a seemingly impossible challenge, and you have the makings of very good strategies for compelling us to eat.

As a toddler, my strong-willed niece Tracy was much too distracted and busy to eat the food her mother fixed for her. Sitting at the dinner table was torture, and after picking at her food, she began to squirm and tried sneaking away from the table. Her dad had tried the you'll-sit-there-until-you-eat-it approach, and her mom had tried the pretend-your-mouth-is-a-hangar-for-the-airplane approach, but Tracy ended up spending hours asleep at the table in front of a full plate of cold food.

Her older sister, Kelli, hit upon a solution without even realizing it. One evening at dinner, Tracy again refused to eat her meat. As her dad began to admonish her, Kelli interrupted. "It's okay, Dad. I don't want her to eat all that meat. I'm the oldest. I don't want Tracy to catch up with me or be stronger than me just because she eats her dinner. Let her go. I'll eat her meat."

Tracy's eyes flashed with surprise and anger. "No way!" she cried. "You can't *have* my meat! I'm *going* to be stronger than you!" As she shoveled her meat into her mouth, her parents looked at each other in amazement.

It seemed like such a transparent and simple ploy. And yet, for the next few months, it took only the slightest reminder that Kelli was stronger than her younger sister to strengthen Tracy's resolve to eat healthy portions. As she got older, of course, the approach no longer worked, but by then she was able to identify even more compelling reasons for eating right: staying fit, competing in soccer, etc.

Sometimes it's not enough to define the goal for your SWC. You must also figure out what it is that will compel him or her to *want* to achieve it.

HELP ME DECIDE WHAT IT WILL TAKE
TO INSPIRE ME

As a typical SWC, I work in bursts of great inspiration, often followed by long plateaus of nothingness. To many, especially frustrated parents, this looks like pure and simple procrastination. But for the SWC, there is a difference between procrastination and a lack of inspiration. The distinction lies in this question: What will it take to inspire me?

Often, simple powers of observation will help you determine what inspires your child. Even if your SWC is a toddler, start watching for the times when he or she seems particularly happy or is focusing a great deal of attention on a specific task. You can pick up a lot of clues without even asking.

Because I travel so much, our sons became frequent fliers early in their lives. Even as toddlers they were drawn to different aspects of the airplane trips. Robert would instantly make friends with the flight attendants and his fellow passengers. Mike, however, immediately began to test whether his seat cushion was indeed a flotation device. When I propose yet another trip to my road-weary sons, I know I have to use different approaches to inspire each boy: Robert needs to hear about new friends and exciting social events; Michael needs the promise of new horizons to discover, unconquered fields to explore.

As soon as your SWC is old enough to understand the reasoning process, you can ask, "What will it take to motivate you to do this?" Be prepared to hear "I don't know" or "Nothing." But don't be discouraged. Your child will know you are serious when you ask again a day or so later and when you seem committed to getting a response.

You must also be prepared for the first answer to be outrageous. The SWC is, after all, trying to see what your reactions will be, and he knows how to get some pretty spectacular ones. So don't be blown away by the first answer to your question. Just look at your child and blink, and wait for him to back down to a reasonable reply. It will almost always happen quickly if your child realizes that you know he is trying to get a rise out of you.

I first wrote about how to motivate your child in my book *Every Child Can Succeed.* Although circumstances may vary, the process for getting to the goal remains consistent, and it's critical for motivating the SWC. Let me illustrate: You want me to keep my room clean. It's a disaster, and nothing seems to motivate me to straighten it. You ask me what I think it will take to get me to keep my room clean. I shake my head and say, "Nothing. I don't want to keep it clean." Bite your tongue and say, "Why don't you think about it, and I'll ask you again tomorrow."

The next day, you ask again. This time I shrug and say, "I don't know." Don't push. Wait another day or two and ask again. This time when you ask I say, "Money. Cash money." You look thoughtful, and ask: "How much money are we talking about?" I quickly reply, "Five thousand dollars." Don't react. Just look and me and blink. If you have to say something, just repeat what I said: "Five thousand dollars."

I say, "Okay…five dollars."

Just like that. I dropped my price. You and I both knew my demand was ridiculous. But instead of ranting and raving, you just looked at me in a way that let me know you're not going to take the bait. So I took what I figured I could actually get.

Now you can close the deal. "Okay," you say. "For the next three weeks, I'll give you five dollars a week if your room stays clean. But after three weeks, you need to think of something besides money that will motivate you to keep your room straightened."

That does two things. First, it prevents you from always having to bribe your SWC with money to get cooperation. Second, it prompts your child to think, *What would it take to get me to do something I don't want to do?*

This step can help you teach your child how to inspire and motivate *himself*. After all, once your child leaves home, chances are no one will volunteer to fill your shoes when it comes to reminders about tasks and motivating and monitoring the SWC's success.

You may be surprised at how well you are received when you simply ask your SWC what it will take to motivate him or her. Parents and teachers often overlook the simple and yet profoundly effective approach of actually talking openly about the issues. You may even need to admit that the task to be done *is* boring and seemingly unnecessary. That said, define the purpose for jumping through this particular hoop, and ask your SWC what will motivate him or her to do it. If your child just can't come up with any ideas, you may need to suggest a few in the beginning. Provide some options, and it won't take long for your SWC to begin supplying his or her own ideas. This can help children learn to think independently, to help motivate themselves, and to design situations and circumstances that will help them achieve their goals.

ASK ME HOW (OR IF) I WANT YOU TO HELP ME

If your SWC understands the purpose and outcome of a particular goal and is committed to achieving it, you can then help identify the methods for accomplishing the task.

If you are not an SWC yourself, you may feel overwhelmed at the prospect of coming up with lots of creative and motivating ideas. Over the years, I've polled many unmotivated SWCs and have gathered some good examples of what has worked for them when they must do things that are difficult, unpleasant, or boring. Here are five of the ideas:

1. Don't assume I want your help.
From the very beginning, my SWC had more than his share of the I'll-do-it-myself independent streak. Mike, even as a toddler, didn't want me always to step in and help him do something he was having trouble doing alone. Helping him open the packaging of a new toy, tie his shoe, put a straw in his soft drink—all of these gestures often elicited loud protests from him unless I asked if he wanted my help. Although I still sometimes forget, I'm finally getting used to asking, "Mike, do you want some help with that?"

2. Get my buy-in on an artificial deadline.
When a large project looms and you realize there is no way your SWC will be able to do everything at the last minute, try establishing an artificial deadline or two. It's important that you and your SWC do this together so that both of you know it's not just a trick or a subtle form of manipulation.

Lay out the project and mutually decide on one or two inter-mediate deadlines for different portions of the task. Determine the dates and the rewards for turning each part of the assignment in by its deadline. Decide whether there will be a penalty for missing the intermediate deadline and what that might be. *The prospect of a reward is more motivating than the threat of a penalty,* so emphasize the positive aspects more than the negative.

3. Use quick, no-big-deal reminders with me.
Ask your SWC how or if he or she wants to be reminded as the various deadlines approach. If your child perceives most of your reminders as nagging, try using a code word. For example, you may both agree that the word *incoming* is all you need to say to remind your SWC that the deadline is almost upon him. Keep the words light and nonthreatening, but stick to the plan and consistently enforce the penalties and rewards. If your child is younger, instead of asking, just start trying different words or phrases and find out what works best.

4. Give advice or suggestions only if I ask.
Believe it or not, we SWCs will welcome your advice and suggestions—as long as we have asked you for them. Keep your offer of advice very informal and even lighthearted. Unsolicited

opinions can get you into a lot of trouble with your SWC and often lead to misunderstanding. Make sure your child is committed to achieving the goal before you offer to help him or her work toward it.

When giving advice, make a conscious effort to empathize by recalling times when you were in a similar situation. Don't reminisce to the point of boring your SWC, just state why you understand the dilemma. As an SWC, I'm more likely to ask for and take your advice if I feel you understand what I'm going through in the first place.

5. Offer me "emergency road service."

If your SWC suddenly runs into a brick wall, you can feel good about providing some emergency resources, but it's a good idea to reinforce the idea of responsibility. Your child can't take off unprepared and count on always being rescued by a nearby tow truck. There is a price to pay for such services.

For example, if your SWC neglected to tell you about all the supplies he would need for a last-minute project, you might agree to go out of your way to get the necessary materials. Then, instead of saying, "Next time, tell me what you need before the day it's due," say, "What can I expect from you that will make me feel better about taking care of this last-minute emergency?"

61

You and your SWC can negotiate the price of these services, whether it be extra chores, an agreement to restructure the next project, etc.

HELP ME CELEBRATE MY SUCCESSES—EVEN THE SEEMINGLY INSIGNIFICANT ONES

There's nothing so motivating as being recognized and appreciated for achieving a difficult goal. Every child benefits when his parents make a concerted effort to find and appreciate what he does best. The behavior and attitude of your SWC will improve as you point out the areas where he or she has made a difference. SWCs want you to notice that we *can* do the impossible if we make up our minds to do it. Let us know you don't doubt our capability even to change the world if we decide to.

My parents never told me I wasn't living up to my potential. They simply looked for opportunities to identify and praise my strengths, and they encouraged me to dream about all the possibilities. They have always lived a modest earthly life, but the legacy they are leaving me is eternal.

Your SWC has great potential. If you begin to look beyond the ordinary places, you may find some incredible treasures!

KEY INSIGHTS FROM THE HEART OF AN SWC

- Teaching me to motivate myself will be more valuable than either of us realizes.
- I sometimes need to experience the consequences of *not doing* something in order to experience the motivation *for doing* it.
- I respond better to a compelling problem that needs to be solved than to a chore that needs to be done.

Do you want to be counted wise,
to build a reputation for wisdom?
Here's what you do:
Live well, live wisely, live humbly.
It's the way you live,
not the way you talk, that counts.

James 3:13

CHAPTER FOUR

So What's the Big Deal About School?

I clearly remember the day I began my teaching career. I taught high-school English, and at twenty-two I was only four years older than some of my students. As a rookie, I got some advice from a couple of seasoned veterans. "Some kids just aren't school material," they told me. "You'll waste a lot of time trying to teach kids who don't want to learn. Just let 'em drop through the cracks and teach the ones who'll listen."

But I had a problem. It didn't take me long to realize that the kids we were "dropping through the cracks" were some of my favorite students. They were bright, creative, and a little obnoxious. They thought school was boring. Actually, so did I—and I was the *teacher!* I couldn't figure out why our educational system was letting so many smart kids go. Shouldn't we be trying to reach them some other way?

Every summer vacation during the eight years I taught in the public schools, I went back to work in the corporate sector. I did it not only for extra income but also for the diverse experience. I wanted to know if I was effectively preparing my students for the world after graduation. That first summer, I made a startling discovery: In the real world, you get hired for the very attributes that get you into trouble at school!

Think about it. The gift of gab, resourcefulness, thinking outside the lines, taking initiative, being independent, figuring out unique angles, using a vivid imagination—all these traits, many common to the SWC, are assets on the job! True, they can make you an inconvenient student in school, but many highly successful people were not "school material." Ask a busy entrepreneur, a top-producing salesperson, or a talented actor what his or her grades were like in school, and you'll often find he doesn't even want to talk about it.

For many SWCs, school is often just a prison sentence to be served, a punishment to be endured. From our SWC perspective, so much of school is drill, repetition, and endless busywork that it isn't worth the trouble to get good grades. For many parents, this poses a great problem as their SWC grows up. Every child is gifted. Every child possesses intelligence. But often, as I've said, the SWC's greatest strengths aren't appreciated in the classroom. I'd like to offer a few insights into why an SWC, like me and many others, may make life troublesome when it comes to academics and classroom behavior.

JUST BECAUSE WE CAN GET AN A DOESN'T MEAN WE WANT TO

What if your SWC child brings home a report card full of D's and F's? Most parents' first reaction is to say, "These grades *have* to come up! If you don't get these grades up, you can't..."

But there are two major problems with this approach:

First, it's unrealistic to expect your child to bring all his or her grades up at once. It's too overwhelming. Besides, all the classes are not equally important to the SWC. If you insist on an all-or-nothing approach, you will almost certainly fail.

Second, the approach assumes that your SWC is as committed as you are to improving his or her grades. That leaves your SWC out of the loop, with no input into his or her own destiny.

As an SWC, I recommend a different approach. Let's say you want to motivate your daughter to improve her grades. Try this scenario:

Holding the report card full of bad grades, talk calmly to your strong-willed daughter. "Hmm, an F in history. Did you want an F in history?" If she nods and says yes, just back off. You can't *make* her want anything higher than an F, at least not for the moment.

Move on. "A D in English. Is that what you wanted to get?" you ask.

She shakes her head. No. You continue. "What grade would you like to get in English?"

"I don't know. I think I'd like to get at least a C."

You nod your head in agreement (even if you'd really like her to go for a higher grade). "What do you think it will take to get a C?"

She rolls her eyes and replies, "A miracle." You smile and say, "Would you like me to help you achieve this miracle?"

From that point, you have established that she is committed to getting a higher grade. You have offered your help but not insisted. From there, you can proceed in several directions, depending on your individual child. If your child tells you he or she doesn't want your help, say you will be available if needed.

Gently remind your child that there are consequences for bad grades: He or she may not qualify for playing a favorite sport, or may not go on that field trip, or may not get car insurance. Stay calm and empathetic. Perhaps briefly recall when you have gone through the same type of circumstance. You obviously need to hold your child accountable, but you can't expect much improvement if your SWC hasn't decided that change needs to occur.

It's hard for most parents to accept that grades earned in school rarely reflect what an SWC has actually learned. Sometimes the best you can do is help your SWC understand that getting the grades may be jumping through hoops in order to attain the goal he or she really wants. Making the grades themselves be the ultimate goal will backfire on you almost every time.

Jason's mom was at the end of her rope. Her sixteen-year-old SWC was flunking out of his economics class, and she told me she'd tried everything to get him to improve the grade: threats, promises, bribes. "Jason can ace that class," she insisted. "But he won't even try!" I knew enough about Jason's mom to have a good idea what the real problem was. She is a smart lady herself and was one of those students who got straight A's in school. She knows her son is intelligent, and at the time she couldn't understand why he wouldn't exert the effort to get a good grade. I also knew Jason well enough to recognize that he was exhibiting a classic SWC behavior. Why spend valuable time studying for a class that he would have no use for in the future?

I asked his mom a couple questions.

"Does Jason need this class to graduate?"

"No," she admitted. "But a failing grade sure won't look good to the college he has decided he wants to attend."

"Have you asked Jason what grade he wants to get in this class?"

She looked surprised. She had never considered working for less than an A in any class. As we talked, Jason's mom forced herself to consider my SWC advice. Here's what worked:

Jason's mom made sure that her son knew the point of taking this class in the first place. In this instance, the point was to keep his transcript looking good for his college applications. Jason hadn't thought about that. He admitted that a D or an F would look pretty bad. His mom (after a big gulp) asked if he'd want to work for at least a C, knowing that a C figured into his grade-point average wouldn't kill his chances for future scholarships.

She suggested that Jason ask his economics teacher what he would have to do in order to get a C by the end of the semester. Jason felt relieved. He knew he wasn't motivated to work for an A in that class. But a C—well, he could do that without much effort. His mom, his teacher, and Jason briefly designed a strategy for getting the C, and Jason went to work.

The pressure for getting an A was off. The point of taking the class was clear. In the end, Jason actually got a B instead of a C, and he admitted he kind of enjoyed the challenge.

IF YOUR SWC REFUSES TO DO HOMEWORK, MAYBE HOMEWORK ISN'T THE ISSUE

How many battles have you fought with your SWC over homework? We SWCs don't relish the idea of doing more schoolwork after we've left the classroom. The idea that we must also devote our spare time to doing something we could barely endure all day seems ridiculous. If you assume we should do the homework just because it's assigned, you will have a battle on your hands almost every time. As I said in the last chapter, more than other kids, SWCs needs an answer to the question *What's the point?*

We SWCs want to know why we should spend time and effort doing something. We're not being smart alecks. We truly want to know the answer to the question. If we understand the purpose of the homework (and sometimes the explanation can be as simple as "it's a necessary hoop to jump through"), we can make a conscious decision as to whether it's worth our efforts to do it.

Remember, SWCs know there are consequences for *not* doing homework. But we also know that we can choose to take the consequences. As much as a parent may not want to think about this, the fact is that you cannot force your SWC to do the homework. We can be motivated, inspired, and held accountable. But we cannot be forced to do homework against our will. Many parents end up doing the work themselves. Some yell and scream and punish, but almost all of those parents end up being the ones who suffer the most. *Your* high blood pressure, *your* headaches, *your* ulcers won't help your SWC get the homework done.

Foster Cline and Jim Fay, in *Parenting with Love and Logic*, put it this way:

> While unwillingness to do homework, bad grades, or
> tardiness at school may be maddening to us, we must
> find a loving way to allow the consequences to do the
> teaching for the child, whatever those consequences
> might be.... The parenting with love and logic
> approach helps kids raise their odds of becoming
> thinking individuals who choose success. As parents,
> this means we must allow for failures and help our

kids make the most of them during their elementary school days, when the price tags are still reasonable.[1]

So what can you do? Here are some suggestions.

1. Establish the reason for doing homework in the first place.
Your SWC will respect the fact that you are as honest as possible in evaluating the purpose. Let's face it: Sometimes homework is a waste of time. It can be boring, repetitious busywork. But the reality is that—right or wrong—often the homework assignments are counted as part of the student's final grade. So help your SWC figure out what needs to be done in order to accomplish the goal he or she sets.

Jason, for example, had determined that he wanted to get at least a C in his economics class. If doing a certain amount of homework is part of the equation, he will need to know that the consequences for not doing his homework could be that he loses the C.

2. If grades themselves are not a motivating factor, find out what is.
Obviously each SWC will be different. For instance, the practice spelling tests and sentence drills were a pain in the neck for my second-grade SWC. He felt he already knew the words, and

if he missed a couple, well, they probably weren't that important anyway. The evenings at home were becoming tense and full
of arguments as Mike kept putting off his homework. Finally, I
took some of my own advice. I know Mike loves checklists and
charts. I asked him to help me design a chart for keeping track
of finished tasks each week. One of those tasks was studying for
his spelling test. He loves checking off the items on the chart,
and now we rarely have an unfinished assignment!

If your SWC is not a chart person, experiment with other
motivators. It may take some time and a few failed experiments
to find an approach that works.

3. Keep a calm, reasonable attitude as much as possible.
Whenever you can, phrase requirements in the form of positive
rather than negative terms. For example, instead of saying: "If
you don't get that homework done by dinner, you won't be watching your favorite television show tonight!" Try: "Your favorite
TV show is on at eight. You'll need to have homework done before
that so you won't miss any of it."

4. Put as much control as you can into the hands of your SWC.
Let your child know what the point of the homework is, what
the consequences of not doing it will be, and then let him or

her decide what to do. You may sometimes have to back off and let your SWC accept the consequences without being rescued at the last minute. When children realize there really is accountability, they usually change their perspective and begin to take responsibility for themselves instead of relying on their parents to rescue them.

HELP YOUR SWC MAINTAIN A GOOD RELATIONSHIP WITH TEACHERS

In chapter two, we discussed the importance of a good relationship between parents and SWCs. This fundamental concept is just as important when it comes to the teacher-student interaction. Even teachers who are boring or uncreative and predictable can still have a positive influence on an SWC if they truly love and value the child.

Respect is definitely a two-way street. If the teacher recognizes and appreciates the strengths of an SWC, that SWC probably won't pose much of a discipline problem. But when a teacher fails to appreciate individual strengths or insists on a rigid and inflexible code of conduct, trouble begins. Here is a classic example:

Josh is a fun-loving SWC in the third grade. His teacher, Mrs. Jones, is strict—a by-the-book disciplinarian. One afternoon during recess, a mischief-maker turned every student desk to face the back of the room. When Mrs. Jones and her class came in, she immediately issued the command. "All right, children, I want you to turn your desks around at once." Every child except Josh quickly turned his or her desk to face the front of the room again.

Josh, after pausing a moment, turned his desk *around*—all the way around—and sat with his back to the teacher. Mrs. Jones could have quickly diffused the situation if she really understood how Josh's mind works. She could have said something like, "Oh, that's cute, Josh. Nice to see your back," and gone on teaching. It would only take a few moments while Josh was getting a few laughs for him to turn his desk around and join the rest of the class. Unfortunately, that's not how it went.

Mrs. Jones was furious. She pointed her finger at Josh and said, "*That's enough,* young man! You turn your desk around and face me this *instant* or you are on your way to the principal's office!" The ultimatum had been issued, and Josh simply shrugged and walked out of the room and headed toward the principal's office.

I'm not advocating letting kids get by with smart-mouth comments that are inappropriate. But Josh wasn't trying to be disrespectful. He struggled all year with Mrs. Jones. He knew how to push her buttons, and she repaid him with nothing but anger and punishment. It didn't have to be that way.

Contrast Josh's experience to Katherine's. Katherine was a troubled thirteen-year-old SWC who had barely survived her parents' divorce. She was a pretty good kid, but adolescence hit her hard. Junior high was dramatically different from elementary school, and the mix of home problems and new social circumstances was proving to be too much. She began to experiment with a little alcohol, a little sex, a few drugs. Her mom was frantic but was also struggling just to keep her own life together.

Katherine began to spiral out of control. Her grades plummeted, her choice of friends caused her family distress, and she defied her mother at every turn. Enter Mrs. Adams. Mrs. Adams was a quiet, unassuming junior-high-school teacher who truly loved kids. Right away she spotted Katherine and made her a special project. Katherine told me a few years later that Mrs. Adams made all the difference in the world when it came to school survival. Here was a teacher who was a tough disciplinarian, who held her students to a high academic standard, and who could motivate Katherine to do whatever she asked her to do.

Why? Mrs. Adams told Katherine how much she loved the way her mind works. She looked for ways Katherine could be successful without having to conform to traditional methods. She

commiserated with Katherine about some of the class requirements that seemed boring or irrelevant. Katherine said later how
much it meant to know that Mrs. Adams would hold her accountable but would never embarrass her or make her feel small.

Katherine began to stay after school voluntarily, helping Mrs.
Adams and talking to her for hours. And because Mrs. Adams
was firm about getting work out of the way before enjoying any
leisure time, Katherine actually did her homework. Katherine
usually didn't want to go home, but Mrs. Adams would gently
nudge her out, telling her how much she looked forward to seeing her the next day. By the end of ninth grade, Katherine had
decided she wanted to be a teacher, and Mrs. Adams was already
helping her plan her strategy for conquering college and beginning her career.

When I first met Katherine a few years ago, she was in her
fourth year of teaching seventh- and eighth-grade math. She said
she loved teaching, but she especially loved getting all the kids
that none of the other teachers wanted. She winked and said, "I
think Mrs. Adams would have liked it that way too!"

So how can you get a teacher for your SWC who's more like
Mrs. Adams than Mrs. Jones? There are no guarantees, but you
have more control than you may think. Despite a lot of bad press
about teachers, you'll find that many of them truly love kids.

There are more demands on a teacher's time and curriculum than ever before, so if you want to help your SWC really get to know his or her teacher and be known, you and your child will need to do most of the leg work. Here are two things you can do:

1. Write a brief profile of your SWC, listing natural strengths and abilities.[2]

When you talk to your SWC's teacher, ask how you and your SWC can help use those strengths to succeed in the classroom. Don't list or dwell on limitations or shortcomings. Your SWC already knows what he or she doesn't do well. Start with and emphasize the positive aspects, and encourage the teacher to help you design ways to overcome challenges in the classroom.

2. Keep an open line of communication between you, your SWC, and the teacher.

Encourage your SWC to speak to the teacher every day, even if it's just to say hello, and make mention of something positive. ("I like the new poster." "That's a cool necklace." "I'm glad you gave us an extra day for the test.") It won't take long for the teacher to begin to notice your SWC and start making positive comments in return. Drop a personal note to the teacher every once in a while, reinforcing how much you appreciate his or her efforts to help kids learn and feel valued. Let the teacher know that you aren't going to let your SWC get by with excuses for not doing work or obeying the rules but that you also want to find as many ways as possible to help your SWC succeed.

Your SWC will watch your relationship with his or her teacher carefully. If you make it a priority to maintain a good one, the chances are much better that your SWC will follow your example. If you do get into a position where you believe your SWC's teacher will simply not be flexible or accepting of your SWC's strengths, you may need to pursue a course that would allow your SWC to change teachers or classroom situations. (For a more detailed explanation of how to do this, read chapter 8 of my book *Every Child Can Succeed*.)

WHAT IF THE TEACHER THINKS YOUR CHILD
HAS A LEARNING DISABILITY?

You know by now that the SWC doesn't fit any particular mold or follow a predictable pattern. SWCs often thrive on change and conflict, and we have a completely different perspective from the average person. We present you with some unique challenges, but we can also provide you with some wonderful insights and innovations. This is problematic when the education system insists that a child adjust and accommodate instead of finding ways to fit the education to the child.

When the SWC resists, he or she may be tested for learning disabilities or behavior disorders. But what if the very traits and characteristics the SWC gets in trouble for are the ones that could potentially change the world? Not long ago, Dr. Peter Breggin quoted *Newsweek* magazine in his book *The War Against Children*. Dr. Breggin said that *Newsweek* had asked the questions: "Where are the great thinkers of the '90s? Where are the Freuds, the Einsteins, the Picassos?" Dr. Breggin then responded with a sobering thought: "What if we're medicating them?"[3]

When you think about it, all three of those great men would have fit most if not all of the symptoms of many learning disorders. Attention deficit disorder (A.D.D.) is being diagnosed so rapidly that the cases are multiplying faster than most schools can dispense the daily dose of medication. The at-risk programs in most school districts are overflowing with candidates who are unsuccessful in the regular classroom. More and more students are participating in pull-out programs, where they must leave the classroom and get individual or specialized help. Legitimate physiological and neurological disorders exist. If a child with a bona fide disability is placed with ten other children who simply have exhibited inconvenient or downright bad behavior, however, that child will not receive the help he truly needs. (One of the best books I have ever read about attention deficit disorder is Thomas Armstrong's *The Myth of the A.D.D. Child: 50 Ways to Improve Your Child's Behavior and Attention Span Without Drugs, Labels, or Coercion.*[4])

Perhaps we need to ask ourselves an important question: If this many kids can't cope with the traditional methods, shouldn't we be changing the methods instead of trying to change the kids? I'm not talking about special privileges or dumbing down the system. I'm talking about deciding what the point of education is, and then finding effective ways to achieve the goal. It's not really such a mystery. In his book *Teaching Through Encouragement*, Robert Martin put forth a simple but profound explanation for why children may not be paying attention: "Inattention is really a way of saying that a student is paying attention to something the teacher isn't interested in. A student who never pays attention is paying attention to something."[5]

If your SWC thinks school is boring anyway and hates doing work that seems to have no point or purpose, is it surprising that he or she may become a candidate for special education? It may have nothing to do with a lack of intelligence or even a lack of ability.

Michael Valentine, a codirector of Children First of the Center for the Study of Psychiatry...has reminded us about the overall failure to research and to promote the most important alternatives of all for children who are restless and inattentive in school—improved instruction and curriculum.[6]

The blame, of course, cannot be laid solely at the educators' feet. Nor can we assume that a child's difficulty is due to a lack of motivation or failure to match learning styles. There are no pat formulas that will give us quick answers to the question of why an SWC is not doing well in school. But it is important that we not assume our child's unconventional behaviors or learning styles are indicative of a disability. It is essential that we determine how much of our SWC's lack of success may be due to a physical, psychological, or educational disorder and how much may be due to the system's failure to recognize and value the way his or her mind works.

You can be your SWC's greatest advocate for his getting the best possible education. You know your child. Help your child's teacher recognize and understand your child's strengths. Don't just throw your hands up and surrender when the school wants to label your SWC. Stay positive but be firm. If you believe that your SWC needs to be evaluated for a learning disability, by all means follow a cautious path. Well-versed pediatricians can help you rule out physical problems first. They can then assist you in finding trustworthy counselors or educators to evaluate the symptoms and find out how much is a matter of learning style and how much goes beyond that.

Keep an open mind, and search until you find a medical professional you can trust, preferably one who has a handle on the differences in learning styles and recognizes the hallmark traits of an SWC. Take down the lines of first resistance before you take more drastic action. (Chapter 8 will provide more details about this.)

You cannot excuse bad behavior; you cannot allow criminal activity; you must not let your SWC by on special exemptions or privileges. By the same token, you dare not assume that something is inherently wrong with your SWC because he or she will not do things your way or a certain educator's way.

KEEP SCHOOL IN PERSPECTIVE

Next time you find yourself arguing with your SWC over homework, grades, and tests, ask yourself how important the whole issue will be ten years from now. Ask yourself what the real issue is—getting the job done, or getting things done your way? Is it worth sacrificing your relationship? Does your SWC know the point?

If you can find ways to identify and use your SWC's natural strengths, you'll find that success may be more attainable than you thought—in school *and* in life!

KEY INSIGHTS FROM THE HEART OF AN SWC

- It doesn't matter how important grades are to you. What matters is how important they are to me.
- Tackle the issue of grades one subject at a time. Don't demand that I improve everything at once.
- Help me discover and commit to compelling reasons to learn in the first place.

It is absolutely clear that God
has called you to a free life.
Just make sure that you don't use this freedom
as an excuse to do whatever you want to do
and destroy your freedom.
Rather, use your freedom
to serve one another in love;
that's how freedom grows.

Galatians 5:13

CHAPTER FIVE

How Can I Best Discipline My Strong-Willed Child?

Michael Tobias, you need to pick up those toys and put them in the basket now!" Even as I heard myself issue the order to my then-four-year-old, I realized I was in trouble. I sometimes forgot, and occasionally still forget, that Mike is just as strong-willed as I am and that I have never reacted well to orders and ultimatums. But I had already climbed out on my limb, and I wasn't about to come back.

Noting that Mike was not obeying, I moved a little farther out on the limb. "Mike, if I have to pick up those toys, I'm going to give them to some other kids." He stood as tall as he could and looked at me. "Give them to some other kids," he said. I couldn't hide my surprise. Some of those toys were among his favorites. But he'd just climbed out on his limb too. Without another word, I scooped up the toys and took them down to the garage. Later that week I gave them to the Compassionate Ministries program at our church. Six months later, Mike had still not asked for any of those toys. He had known what the price was, and he had been fully prepared to pay it.

If you have an SWC, I don't have to tell you that discipline strategies that work for other kids simply don't have the same effect on the SWC. From the cradle to the grave, your SWC will present you with challenges unlike those from your other children. The fact that you are the big person and your SWC is the small person is not enough. You cannot rule based on rank or privilege or even brute strength.

We SWCs respect authority and expect accountability and discipline. We don't expect you to let us get by with bad behavior or give us special privileges if we don't deserve them. The strategies in this chapter can help you accomplish important bottom-line goals with your SWC without sacrificing that accountability. But you'll need to keep an open mind. You'll need to be willing to try new approaches. And you'll need to understand why you never have to relinquish your authority when you decide to share control with the SWC, who can't live without it. Give it a try—you have nothing to lose. You've probably tried everything else. You may be amazed at the results when you try what we SWCs suggest!

Whenever I speak or write about discipline, I emphasize another basic parenting principle:

YOU CAN ENFORCE RULES, BUT YOU CAN'T FORCE COMPLIANCE

When I became the mother of twins, I made a startling and frustrating discovery. Although those babies were less than seven pounds each, there were still certain things I simply could not force them to do! I couldn't make them sleep through the night or eat on my timetable or keep their diapers clean. As they grew, I realized I couldn't force them to respect me or love me or even obey me without question.

Like it or not, each of us has a free will. As parents, we must realize that we cannot force our children to obey simply because we demand it. If you frequently find yourself arguing and engaging in power struggles with your SWC, take stock of how you communicate what you want. Are you taking into account the fact that your SWC has a choice to obey you? If you yell and scream about how your child had better do what you say *or else*, he or she will just tune you out.

In the church where I grew up, we often sang: "Trust and obey, for there's no other way to be happy in Jesus, but to trust and obey." I surrendered my life to God at an early age. I know the importance of obedience, and I don't argue with the concept at all. But I always pictured that song being sung through gritted teeth by people who were suggesting I had no choice but to trust and obey. But God doesn't force anyone to serve Him. I picture myself sitting at a table with God and Him telling me, "Okay, here's the deal. If you choose this, that happens; if you choose that, this happens..." And I *comply*. To me, *comply* means *obey* because I have a choice. I can choose eternal life or death—but God gives me the choice. I don't serve Him because I fear the consequences of disobeying. I serve Him because I can have a relationship with almighty God. My personal version of this song goes: "Trust and comply, and I won't ask why. I'll be happy in Jesus; I'll just trust and comply."

Again, you may think this is ridiculous. I should just get over my strong will and obey. But it's no small thing to us SWCs. You may assume your statements are just "directives" or "suggestions," but we SWCs often hear them as orders issued for the purpose of gaining control over us.

THE PROBLEM ISN'T AUTHORITY, BUT HOW
AUTHORITY IS COMMUNICATED

A critical point for you to understand is that most of us SWCs accept our parents or teachers as authority figures in our lives. We wouldn't respect you if you didn't hold the line. We would feel insecure if you failed to hold us accountable to the boundaries you've set. But we don't want you to be the boss. We want you to assume the best of us while providing us with guidelines and rules.

I explain this with what I call my drive-through theory. When I stop at a fast-food drive-through and give my order to the little box, I often hear something like "That will be $3.86. Please drive forward." *Please drive forward.* Isn't that a keen sense of the obvious? Give me a break! Do they think I'm too stupid to know I'm supposed to drive forward to the window?

By the time I get up to the cashier, I'm so irritated I never want to come back. On the other hand, when I hear "That will be $3.86 at the first window, please," I know exactly what I am supposed to pay and exactly where I am supposed to go. But it's said in a way that assumes I am a smart and capable person. I know I can't get food without paying. I know I can't just pay whatever I feel like. There's an exact price and an exact location, and I don't argue with that. It's how you *get* me there that makes all the difference. Now that may not seem like a big deal to you, but it's essential that SWCs get credit for recognizing the obvious.

In many cases, parents don't realize that what they intend as a simple directive (*go to bed, sit down, stop hitting your brother*) can be taken as an absolute ultimatum by the SWC. For years I have avoided patronizing a particular restaurant in our community. The reason? A neon sign in the window says, *Get in here!* My objection seems ridiculous to some of my friends, but I resent the command. What the marketing department thinks is cute, I think is insulting. Another organization specializing in family products used the motto *Go Home!* Although they were trying to command attention, it created a certain amount of hostility. In several southern states numerous highway billboards advertise venues and huge red letters that simply say, *Exit Now*. My husband sees this as a friendly reminder of which exit he needs to take, but my strong-willed mind hears it as an imperial order: *Get off the highway now—and I mean it!* So when it's my turn to drive, I pass by the exits with those billboards. I wait until I get to a friendlier exit and work my way back however I have to.

If you are not an SWC, it probably seems ludicrous that SWCs would actually choose to cut off our nose to spite our face. Why would we do things the hard way when we know what the easy way is? I can't give you a rational explanation. All I can tell you is that your SWC will rarely respond well to a direct order. We don't need much modification—*Come on in here; Let's go home; This is your exit*—but we do want you to communicate with respect.

This is different from letting up or backing off of consequences for wrongdoing. You do not let your child off the hook if you modify your requests. The strength of your convictions as the parent helps your child feel secure. Your enforcement of the rules prevents your children from becoming spoiled brats. But how you choose to communicate your message makes all the difference in the world. In *Parenting with Love and Logic*, Foster Cline and Jim Fay illustrate this best in their examples of "Fighting Words" versus "Thinking Words."

- Child says something loud and unkind to the parents:
  FIGHTING WORDS: "Don't you talk to me in that tone of voice!"
  THINKING WORDS: "You sound upset. I'll be glad to listen when your voice is as soft as mine."

- Child is dawdling with her homework:
  FIGHTING WORDS: "You get to work on your studying!"

THINKING WORDS: "Feel free to join us for some television when your studying is done."

- Two kids are fighting:
  FIGHTING WORDS: "Be nice to each other. Quit fighting."
  THINKING WORDS: "You guys are welcome to come back as soon as you work that out."

- Child won't do his chores:
  FIGHTING WORDS: "I want that lawn cut *now!*"
  THINKING WORDS: "I'll be taking you to your soccer game as soon as the lawn is cut."[1]

It may take some practice to rephrase your instructions or commands. Think about what you and your SWC argue about most. Choose the top three, and write them down. For each one, write the phrase you usually hear yourself saying in the heat of the battle. Now try writing a more "thinking" phrase to use as an alternative.

For example, my SWC and I used to argue about whether he was taking too long in his morning shower. After evaluating it, I realized my *fighting* words were, "Mike, it's time to get out of the shower now."

His reply? "No!"

I tried *thinking* words: "Mike, are you ready to get out now?"

"No!"

I tried again. "Two more minutes, okay?"

Immediately he agreed. "Okay."

Even though searching for the right phrase takes extra effort, it will be worth it when your SWC begins to cooperate with you instead of resisting your authority.

YOUR ACTIONS WILL ALWAYS BE MORE EFFECTIVE THAN YOUR EMOTIONS

Almost every SWC I've ever asked has told me their parents yelled at them—a lot. Certainly parents of SWCs often have good reasons for becoming angry and upset with their children's behavior. But anger is usually the *least* effective way to change an SWC's attitude or behavior. If you allow your anger to control your use of discipline techniques, you are almost certainly doomed to failure. I discovered this truth before I even had an SWC of my own.

When I was in training as a police officer, both the police-academy instructors and my field training officers were clear about the process of writing traffic tickets. The rule of thumb was this: When you observed a traffic violation and pulled the violator over, you made the decision whether to give a ticket or just a warning before you ever spoke to the driver. The theory behind that was, of course, that if you did not let your emotions determine your course of action you could not be controlled by either the violator or the circumstances of the violation. Although this was sound in theory, I was not the only rookie who had a difficult time putting it into practice.

One day I saw a driver make an illegal U-turn. Although his action did not endanger anyone in the light traffic, I needed to let him know that what he did was not allowed and certainly posed a potential danger when the traffic was heavier. As the driver pulled over to the side of the road and I parked my patrol car carefully behind him, I had already made up my mind that I would simply give him a stern verbal warning and try to impress upon him that he should never do this again. I was sure I would make his day by letting him out of a potentially expensive traffic ticket.

Before I could even ask him for his driver's license and registration, the driver leaped out of his car and began yelling obscenities at me. "Why did you pull *me* over?" he screamed. "Don't you have anything better to do than to pick on decent citizens? Why aren't you arresting *criminals?*" I must admit, his rage took me by surprise. Before I could answer him, he pointed his finger in my face and looked directly into my eyes. "I didn't do anything wrong, and you can't give me a ticket!" he claimed. My own emotions got the better of me. I must confess that I not only gave him a ticket for the illegal U-turn, but I also added a couple of other miscellaneous but legitimate violations I normally would have overlooked.

The tension escalated beyond reason, and I called for backup. We ended up having to arrest the driver for obstructing justice and assaulting a police officer. If I had stuck to the original deal, I probably could have diffused the conflict. But my own stubbornness and strong will made me unwilling to back down in the heat of the moment. As I gained experience and better judgment, I learned to temper my reactions and keep most volatile situations from blowing up in my face. This has turned out to be one of the most valuable lessons I could have learned before dealing with my own SWC.

SWCs know how to push the buttons. We know how to throw you off balance and then intercept the control. If you allow your own anger and strong will to enter the argument, you've lost already. You are never stronger than when you are calm and in control of your emotions—especially your anger. You do not let your SWC off the hook. You do not let him think his misbehavior is not a big deal. Consequences stay intact. But how you react in any given situation is crucial. One of my very favorite passages in Dr. Dobson's book *The Strong-Willed Child* sums up this issue of emotions versus action with another police example:

Standing on the street corner is a lone policeman who has not been given the means to arrest you. He has no squad car or motorcycle; he wears no badge, carries no gun, and can write no tickets. All he is commissioned to do is stand on the curb and scream insults as you speed past. Would you slow down just because he shakes his fist in protest? Of course not! You might wave to him as you streak by. His anger would achieve little except to make him appear comical and foolish.

On the other hand, nothing influences the way Mr. Motorist drives more than occasionally seeing a black-and-white vehicle in hot pursuit with nineteen red lights flashing in the rear-view mirror. When his car is brought to a stop, a dignified, courteous patrolman approaches the driver's window. He is six foot nine, has a voice like the Lone Ranger, and carries a sawed-off shotgun on each hip. "Sir," he says firmly but politely, "our radar unit indicates you were traveling sixty-five

miles per hour in a twenty-five-mile zone. May I see
your driver's license, please?" He opens his leather-
bound book of citations and leans toward you. He has
revealed no hostility and offers no criticisms, yet you
immediately go to pieces. You fumble nervously to
locate the small document in your wallet (the one with
the horrible Polaroid picture). Why are your hands
moist and your mouth dry? Why is your heart thump-
ing in your throat? Because the course of *action* that
John Law is about to take is notoriously unpleasant.
Alas, it is his *action* which dramatically affects your
future driving habits.[2]

Your emotional reactions, especially in negative circumstances,
will have almost no positive effect on your SWC. Your actions,
on the other hand, can make a profound and lasting impression.

IT'S ALL IN THE WORDS YOU USE...

In the earlier example of fighting words versus thinking words,
it's easy to see the best way to phrase your directives. But they're
not as easily identifiable in the heat of conflict. Often parents of
an SWC don't realize they have thrown down the gauntlet by the

words they said. They don't mean to lay down the law, even if that is the SWC's perception. It takes practice to rephrase your words so that a conflict is diffused instead of escalated. Here are three strategies that may help:

1. If you have a good relationship with your SWC, try using a code word.

Make an agreement that every time your words sound like an ultimatum or edict from on high, your SWC can use a code word. Then you have the opportunity to stop and evaluate how you said something. For example, the code word might be *ouch*. As you are talking to your SWC, she says "Ouch!" and you say "What? What did I say that was so bossy?" She repeats back to you what she perceived as the offense. At that point you can either defend your choice of words or back up and start again. This is not perceived as weakness in the eyes of an SWC. In fact, this may be one of the most effective methods you use for building and keeping his or her respect for you and your authority.

2. Avoid phrases like "you must," "you have to," or "there's no way you're going to."

Even the most cooperative SWC will not surrender complete control. If you say "you *will* do this," I may choose not to do it just to prove that you can't make me. I'm not just trying to be a smart aleck or a rebel. I just want you to know that I have control over what I will and will not do. Again, the phrasing makes a crucial difference.

If it sounds exhausting and overwhelming to think constantly about how your words are being perceived by your SWC, it is. I admit it, and so does every SWC I've talked to. We don't make it easy on you. But this whole book is dedicated to helping you find practical strategies that can help you cope quickly and communicate without having to think through every word.

3. Use the magic word okay.

The word *okay* works miracles. Using it helps a parent maintain authority while still sharing at least a portion of control. This "magic word" doesn't work with everyone, but it is usually effective more than 80 percent of the time with the SWC.

Listen to the difference:

"Tracy, put your seat belt on."

"No."

"I said put your seat belt on."

"No."

Now where do you have to go? Nowhere but a knock-down-drag-out power struggle where everyone loses.

But try this:

"Tracy, put your seat belt on, okay?"

"No."

"Why not?"

"It's too tight—I don't like it."

"Well, we'll loosen it a little, then put it on, okay?"

"Okay." Eight times out of ten.

It's amazing but true—a small point of negotiation usually makes the difference. The *okay?* lets an SWC know that you realize she does always have a choice. Of course, *okay?* doesn't mean, "You don't have to do it." It means, "You can choose the consequences if you want to," which leaves just enough control in the SWC's hands.

GIVE AWAY CONTROL AND GAIN PARENTAL AUTHORITY

In *Parenting with Love and Logic,* Foster Cline and Jim Fay address the issue of how much parents can really control:

Control is a curious thing. The more we give away, the more we gain. Parents who attempt to take all the control from their children end up losing the control they sought to begin with. These parents invite their children to fight to get control back.

In the battle for control, *we should never take any more than we absolutely must have*; we must always cut our kids in on the action. When we do that, we put them in control on our terms. We must give our children the control we don't need to keep the control we do.[3]

Remember that control is not the same as authority. You can and *should* maintain parental authority, but you can do that best by approaching your SWC in a way that shows respect. You want us to know where the lines are drawn, and we want you to know we can step over that line and choose the consequences if we want to. You can show respect for your SWC's free will at the same time you communicate accountability.

For example, when it's time for three-year-old Lisa to take her nap, you say, "Lisa, it's time for your nap, sweetheart. Would you like to take it in your bed or mine?" You firmly state the requirement and give at least two options.

Lisa shakes her head. "No. I don't *want* to take a nap."

Now you state the point: "You need to rest, at least for a little while, even if you don't close your eyes. Where do you want to be that will help you stay quiet and still?" Of course, no approach works all the time, but you may be surprised to see how many arguments won't even have a chance to get started when you give your SWC some control.

KEEP YOUR SENSE OF HUMOR

There is a story told of a duck that walked into a grocery store. He walked up to the grocer.

"You got any grapes?" he asked.

"No," replied the grocer. The duck walked out.

A few minutes later, he walked back in. "You got any grapes?" he asked.

The grocer frowned. "I *told* you. I don't have any grapes."

The duck nodded, and walked out.

A few minutes later, he walked back in. "You got any grapes?" he asked again.

The grocer's face got red, and he leaned over the counter and looked at the duck angrily. "Look—I've told you three times now. I don't have any grapes. If you come in and ask me that question again, I'm going to *nail* your little webbed feet to the *floor.* Do you understand?" The duck shrugged and walked out.

A few minutes later, he walked back in. "You got any nails?" he asked.

The grocer tried to contain his anger. "No!"

The duck looked around. "Got any grapes?"

The SWC doesn't give up easily! Instead of resenting us for it, enjoy it once in a while. We're always thinking, always trying to stay a few steps ahead of you. You can lighten up on your SWC without letting up on your expectations. Enjoy the fact that you have a unique and wonderful child full of surprises and talents. Guide us, but don't force us to follow you too closely. Respect works both ways, and if you earn your SWC's respect, you'll find that discipline might not be as big an issue in the future as it has been in the past.

KEY INSIGHTS FROM THE HEART OF AN SWC

- It's important for me to understand the reasons for a rule or limitation.
- The action you take will be much more effective than the anger you show.
- Negative reinforcement usually has no positive effect on me.

Make a careful exploration of who you are
and the work you have been given,
and then sink yourself into that.
Don't be impressed with yourself.
Don't compare yourself with others.
Each of you must take responsibility
for doing the creative best you can with your own life.

Galatians 6:4-5

CHAPTER SIX

Finding the Right Career: What Will They Do with the Rest of Their Lives?

I was young and enthusiastic when I started my student-teaching position at a suburban high school. I was so excited about spending time with actual students that it didn't occur to me other teachers might not share my zeal. My first day of lunch in the teachers' lounge caught me completely by surprise.

As I sat in the middle of all the seasoned professionals, I expected to overhear pearls of wisdom, bits of advice, and voices of experience. Instead, I heard several murmurs of discontent about the "system" and more than a few complaints about specific students and classroom conditions. One middle-aged teacher stood up to refill his coffee cup. "I hate the whole system," he groused. "I hate the kids and I hate the paperwork, and I especially hate the new training requirements."

I didn't know enough to keep quiet, so I let my incredulous expression show when I spoke to him. I wasn't being impertinent, but I wanted to ask him an important question. "If you hate teaching so much," I said, "why don't you quit and do something you like?" It was his turn to be surprised. Then he gave me a contemptuous look. "You're just a rookie," he snorted. "You'll catch on. I'm forty-five years old, and I'm vested in the retirement system. I've got steady pay, three months off in the summer, and health benefits for my family. Why would I want to start all over now?"

I didn't reply, but it was a clarifying moment. Suddenly I realized how vital it was that I never be trapped in a job. I vowed that I would not allow myself to focus on my career so narrowly that I couldn't leave when I stopped being passionate about what I was doing.

The jobs I had each summer while I was teaching were usually through a temporary employment agency. I honed my secretarial abilities and began learning new skills by volunteering for a wide variety of jobs. I worked as a statistical typist for a trucking company, a marketing assistant for a large advertising agency, an inventory taker for a gaming company, a driver for a limousine-rental company. I held dozens of other positions as well, each offering a unique perspective that contrasted with my teaching job.

Over the next several years, I was able to tell my students the same thing at the beginning of each school year: "I could be a lot of different places doing a lot of different things. I'm here teaching you because I want to be here more than anywhere else. As soon as I want to be somewhere else more than I want to be here, I owe it to you and I owe it to myself to leave."

I have since found that I share this view with most of my SWC friends and colleagues. There's something about our nature that makes us chafe with restlessness when we feel trapped by a job that bores or frustrates us. Work is not simply an obligation we fulfill or a duty we carry out because we must put food on the table. We need to be compelled, fulfilled, challenged.

If you are not an SWC, this may sound unrealistic to you. You may insist that SWCs need to "get a grip" and "learn to live in the real world." After all, what are the chances that your SWC could actually get that perfect job? Well, what if it *could* happen? Wouldn't you rather prepare your SWC to get the job of his dreams than prepare him to settle for whatever he can get?

I was once a guest on a call-in radio show in upstate New York. We had been talking about a variety of ways that kids don't fit in school, especially the highly active and extremely restless SWC. I strongly advocated directing the SWC's high energy level instead of trying to temper it. One irate caller disagreed. "My second-grade daughter is on the move all the time," he said. "I make her be still because I tell her that someday she's going to have a job where she can't just move around any time she wants to."

I just had two questions for him. "Sir, are you calling me from work right now?"

"Yes," he replied.

"Where are you calling me from?" I inquired.

There was a moment's pause before he answered. "My truck. Never mind—I get your point."

Why are we so certain that our SWCs will be destined to work in careers they don't like and aren't suited for? Certainly we need to train our children to stretch outside their comfort zone and be disciplined enough to do things they may not particularly enjoy. But why don't we spend more time helping them discover what they are naturally drawn to and what they can do that will truly be enjoyable for them?

There are many ways to help identify and appreciate which strengths will be most appropriate for which careers in your SWC's future. The common denominator seems to be summed up in one word: diversification. SWCs thrive when we have lots of options, so it stands to reason that the best preparation for adulthood will be to help your SWC learn many skills, explore multiple job opportunities, and conquer many challenges. It's never too early to begin, and as many recent career-search books can verify, it's never too *late* to start. Let's take a look at some practical ways you can help your SWC discover his or her future interests, from early childhood through the teen years.

PREPARE THEM FOR THE BEST OF THEIR LIVES

Early Childhood

Encourage exploration from the beginning. Let your SWC wander freely among the possibilities and show you what naturally captures his or her interest. When our boys were toddlers, they stayed at Grandma's house every day while I worked. Although they were barely walking and talking, we noticed they had a real thirst for knowledge. They were curious about everything. But the twins were already so different from each other that we didn't want to insist they both always did the same thing. So we went down to an educational-supplies store and bought several inexpensive posters—days of the week, months of the year, animal alphabets, the solar system, neighborhood helpers, etc. We posted the charts throughout Grandma's house at eye level for the boys.

Over the next few weeks we watched my sons and answered their questions. Each boy would approach one of the charts, point, and say, "What's that?" We would tell him, and then he would either pursue more questions or walk away without further interest. We applied no pressure for them to learn what was on the posters, and yet both boys eagerly wanted to learn. Robert was drawn to neighborhood helpers and to other people-oriented charts. Michael, on the other hand, focused carefully on the solar system and categorizing the months in a year.

We were setting the stage for encouraging the boys to pursue their interests instead of simply enduring a uniform, prescribed routine.

Start keeping a journal to share with your child when he or she is older. Even if you only jot down a few things once a week, start keeping track of your SWC's likes and dislikes, interests, aversions, etc. Sometimes the smallest detail can help your SWC recognize strengths and preferences. As he or she gets older, share your journal entries and verify your observations. Discuss what you both think might be good indicators of future success. You both may be amazed at how accurate your evaluations will turn out to be.

My sister is five years younger than I am and, as I've already said, has a considerably more compliant personality. When she was just a toddler, I had already started school. Each day when I came home, I sat her down in our playroom and taught her what I had learned at school. My mother noticed right away that Sandee had a sharp mind and was a quick study. Mom provided the toys we seemed to want the most—a blackboard, a small school desk, crayons, paper, and books. We played for hours, and Sandee learned to read and do math well before she started kindergarten. In fact, she had been in first grade for just six weeks when the principal suggested she simply skip the rest and start second grade immediately. At the tender ages of seven and two, my sister and I had already shown our parents what would turn out to be vital clues to our future careers. My sister is a valuable manager for a real estate and property management company, and I ended up teaching!

Elementary School

When your SWC reaches school age, encourage him or her to keep a journal or to somehow keep track of his best successes and most frustrating disappointments. As soon as my sons started school, we began to ask the same two questions every day when they got home: "What did you like about school today?" and "What did you *not* like about school today?" Although many days their answers were predictable (liked recess, didn't like what was served for lunch), we often gained insight into what made them happy and what they were already learning to dread. If your SWC will keep a journal, suggest he or she write down the highs and lows of the day or week. If you have a reluctant communicator, try using a dry-erase board or a blackboard and have your SWC complete these two sentences by the end of each day: "The best thing about my day was..." and "The worst thing about my day was..."

The most important goal is to keep the line of communication open between your SWC and you. Again, save the daily or weekly entries and periodically review them with your SWC. It's not only a good reminder of the past, but a strong indicator of what will make them happy in the future!

The Teen Years

During the teen years, start putting a positive emphasis on community service. Look for opportunities for your SWC to volunteer his skills and talents in ways that make the world a better place while he tests his interest levels and expertise. Dozens of interesting organizations—such as hospitals, police departments, libraries, nursing homes, and food banks—welcome volunteers while providing on-the-job experience. If you have a hard time motivating your SWC to use some energy productively, try matching the hours he or she spends volunteering with opportunities to spend the same number of hours doing something he values, like learning to drive the car, having free time, or shopping with friends. The more variety you encourage in the course of doing the volunteer work, the broader your SWC's experiences will be.

Be sure to discuss each job and to help your SWC identify its best and worst aspects. Talk about where the opportunities could lead, but be sure as well to emphasize the value of doing the work just for the sake of making a difference. Encourage your SWC to keep a brief journal as he or she tries the many options. Again, if your SWC resists writing things down, try the quick-response dry-erase board or blackboard that was suggested earlier.

HOW WILL THEY FIND THE JOBS THEY LOVE?

Hundreds of books are designed to help both young and old find the perfect career. Interest inventories, seminars, and a multitude of other assessments can help pinpoint appropriate career possibilities. By the time your SWC has reached high school, he or she should have a good idea of what is appealing and what is least interesting. The process of a career search need not be complicated or overwhelming, and for the SWC it certainly shouldn't be permanent. Often rather than buying and reading pages and pages of job-hunting advice, your SWC can receive greater benefit from a direct and simple approach. Here are five caveats to keep in mind as you help guide your SWC in the right direction:

1. Don't count on your SWC wanting what you would want.
Each of us is unique. Moreover, your SWC may deliberately choose something different in response to your apparent preferences or pushiness. Consciously back off, and whenever possible, limit your suggestions to answering your SWC's questions. Feel free to ask your SWC if he or she would like your help, but don't take offense if the first answer is no.

2. Chances are good that your SWC will change careers several times during his or her lifetime.
SWCs are at the forefront of current trends dictating that most people will pursue at least three or four careers before retirement. Your SWC will almost never settle for staying in one job doing only one thing for the duration of his or her working years—whether trendy or not. SWCs have little patience for staying in a job we suddenly tire of or that eventually becomes tedious or difficult. Work must seem more akin to play in order for us to stick with it. Similarly, SWCs don't usually hesitate to jump from

job to job if necessary. We often believe that anything is better than our present stressful position, and we'll bail out without a parachute. We are more willing to do distasteful jobs temporarily than to remain in unpleasant circumstances until we find a new permanent position.

3. Your SWC doesn't mind "jumping through hoops" to get to where he or she needs to be.

Your SWC will indeed jump through hoops to achieve a goal, but this is true only so long as both you and he recognize that they are just hoops, not something he is being forced to do. Even the most impatient and carefree SWC might suddenly buckle down and ace chemistry or calculus because that's what it will take to get into the graduate school he or she wants to attend. But we don't do things because you or society say we must. We do those things because we are committed to the goals we decide are worth achieving.

4. Your SWC may be prone to go for what looks good at the moment.

Whenever you can help your SWC recognize what a particular job actually entails, it can save a lot of grief. For example, perhaps your SWC has considered only the more glamorous aspects of being a neurosurgeon—the money, the prestige, the life-and-death responsibility. Maybe you, or a friend who is a neurosurgeon, could find a gentle way of letting your SWC discover how much training is required, how much detail and work goes into the preparation, how much stress and how many potential rules and litigation threats are involved in the day-to-day grind. Never discourage your SWC from believing he or she can achieve something through hard work, but do help your SWC decide whether any goal is worth the required sacrifices.

5. Your SWC believes anything is possible.

You may think your arguments about getting good grades ("you need them to get into college") will motivate your SWC to work harder. Most SWCs, however, don't take the threat seriously ("I'll get into college some other way"). Once we actually make up our minds to do something, we'll move heaven and earth to do it.

AT THE BOTTOM LINE, THEY'VE GOT TO TRY THINGS THEMSELVES

If you're doing your best to help your SWC find and use his or her strengths and talents, don't get uptight about finding the right niche immediately. By our very nature, we SWCs often must use a trial-and-error approach to make sure we're headed in the right direction. At times we may simply take a time-out and deliberately do something that doesn't further any career. In these instances especially, the more pressure you put on us, the less productive we will be. If you truly want to help us find an enjoyable career path, allow us detours and pit stops along the way. Instead of pointing out the need to keep moving, do your best to keep emphasizing the most positive aspects of our nature: determination, tenacity, and resourcefulness.

Chances are good that your SWCs hold the power to literally change the world. Be sure they are headed in the right direction when they do it!

KEY INSIGHTS FROM THE HEART OF AN SWC

- It's important for me to feel I always have options.
- I need to change my environment and vary my challenges frequently.
- I don't want to be like everyone else.

But by shifting our focus
from what we do to what God does,
don't we cancel out all our careful
keeping of the rules
and ways God commanded?
Not at all.
What happens, in fact,
is that by putting that entire way of life
in its proper place, we confirm it.

Romans 3:30-31

CHAPTER SEVEN

What About the Line Between Right and Wrong?

I once conducted an SWC seminar for a group of Christian-radio advertising executives in the beautiful library of a grand Christian institution. As we discussed the characteristics of the SWC, Jay, one of the executives, leaped to his feet and grabbed the large family Bible that was lying close by.

"You're talking about the carnal nature!" he cried. "This strong-willed stuff is just *sin*, pure and simple!" The rest of us were surprised at his vehemence.

"Whoa!" I said quickly. "Sin comes in *all* styles and sizes. No one personality or learning style has a corner on anything good or anything bad." He shook his head, still holding the big black Bible.

"But you're supposed to *obey*," he protested. "God doesn't compromise and negotiate and let you off the hook just because you don't want to follow the rules!"

I nodded. "You're right. He doesn't. But God is the One who designed us with a free will in the first place. Doesn't it stand to reason that He would work within His own parameters? I believe God wants to *use* the strong will He placed in so many of us. Sin is still sin, whether it is being committed by a compliant person or a strong-willed person. The strong will is not the issue. It's the line between what's right and wrong."

Jay did not look completely convinced. One of his SWC colleagues chimed in. "Jay, I don't work the way you do at all, but both of us are successful at our jobs. I know my strong will gets me in trouble sometimes, and I have to make things right, both with God and the person I wronged. But you've gotten in trouble once in a while too. And you're *not* the classic strong-willed child!"

Jay nodded and started to smile. "Yeah. Actually, *I* got in trouble because I came across as being too rigid and inflexible to accept my client's wild ideas." He put the Bible down and took his seat again. "Okay, I get your point. But I still think you strong-willed folks sin a lot more often than I do." He was grinning as the guy next to him jabbed an elbow into Jay's ribs.

Contrary to what some popular theories propose, I believe (as do most of the SWCs I have talked to) that there *are* absolutes. I do not ascribe to the idea of right and wrong being relative. It's especially difficult for SWCs, however, to get along with people who think they are the only ones able to discern what qualifies as right and wrong.

Parents and teachers often tell me that they believe that SWCs delight in breaking rules and getting away with doing wrong things. That is not an SWC trait. That is *sin,* and *anyone* can do that. Again, let me take you into the mind of an SWC when it comes to following the rules. You need to know two things:

1. RULES ARE BASICALLY GUIDELINES

For those who believe it's important not to rock the boat, nor to resist what traditionally works, the actions of the SWC can look suspiciously like disobedience and rebellion. To most SWCs, rules are basically guidelines. It's not arrogance on our part—we just believe we are capable of figuring out what the point of a rule is, and sometimes we use another method of abiding by it.

For example, if I drive into the school parking lot for an evening PTA meeting and the closest parking places are marked

Bus Zone—No Parking, I interpret that sign to mean "If the buses need these spaces, you can't park here; if the buses do *not* need them, you can park here." It's a *guideline!* On the other hand, you won't find a stronger advocate than I am when it comes to making sure the *Handicapped Only* parking is strictly enforced. The reason behind that particular rule is sound, and I don't consider the issue negotiable.

Another good example has now become my classic "stroller story." I first told the story in my book *The Way They Learn.* My rule-conscious sister, Sandee, and I were shopping in a department store a few years ago. Sandee's youngest daughter was still a toddler, and we had her in a stroller. As we got ready to go to the second floor in the store, I took charge of the stroller and started to step onto the escalator. "Wait!" Sandee cried. "Look at that sign! It says *No Strollers on the Escalator.*"

I stared at her. "Are the stroller police going to arrest me?" I asked. "Sandee, that sign is for people who don't know how to safely *put* a stroller on an escalator. Since I *do*, it doesn't apply to me." I swiftly took Allison out and held her securely in my arms as the empty stroller rode beside me on the escalator. My sister did not even follow me for a few minutes. She was horrified that I would so blatantly disregard a rule. But to me, it was simply a guideline.

A few weeks later, I found out I wasn't the only one who interpreted the stroller law this way. As I descended a Dallas–Fort Worth Airport escalator, I noticed a young couple ascending with a huge baby buggy. Even from a distance, I could tell the wife was reading her husband the riot act for bringing the prohibited buggy on the escalator. As I passed them, I heard the husband say to his wife, "Did anybody die? Nobody *died!*"

When you set parameters for the behavior of an SWC, you need to be clear with your reasons for rules and regulations. We do not set out to break rules just out of meanness. Often, though, we end up breaking rules or disobeying because we feel we have no other choice. Perhaps the rule seems pointless. Perhaps the result of obeying will hurt someone else or compromise our beliefs. Perhaps the restrictions seem designed to simply let another person exercise power over us. If you become heavy-handed in your approach and simply start issuing orders to be obeyed, *everyone* is headed for trouble.

2. SWCS WILL NOT BE MANIPULATED

The second thing you need to know is that SWCs demand honesty above all else. We will not be manipulated. We want you to be up-front with us. Don't pretend to be who you're not or promise what you can't deliver. We have a highly sensitive detection device that can instantly pick up signals of insincerity or artificiality. If we feel at all manipulated, we can pull out all the stops and beat you at your own game.

When I was teaching high-school English, a particular department supervisor caused me a great deal of stress and frustration. He was, in my opinion, arrogant and self-important. He loved being in charge and often flaunted his authority, especially over younger women teachers. One day at lunch, he asked me if I had used a particular set of textbooks that were in the book room. I told him I hadn't, since the books were on the supplemental textbook list and I didn't feel they were appropriate to my lessons. He frowned and shook his head. "Listen, Cindy," he said sternly. "I want you to use those textbooks."

Trying to remain respectful, I replied, "Roger, they are not on the required list, and I don't like them."

He leaned closer to me and put on his most menacing look. "Cindy, as your department head, I am *ordering* you to use those books."

After a moment's pause, I nodded my head. "Sure, Roger. I'll use those books this week." His expression was smug and self-satisfied as I walked out of the room.

Later that day, I went to the book room and carried the now-required textbooks to my classroom. After class had started, I handed a book to each student and instructed them to please stand up. After they were standing, I asked them to please place the textbook on their seat and then sit back down. Although they were a little puzzled, they did as I requested. I had my students sit on the books all during class. At the end of the period, I collected them again and put them back in the book room. Fortunately, my students were used to my sometimes unusual behavior, so no one demanded an explanation.

A few days later, Roger cornered me in the lunchroom. "Did you use those books I told you to?" he asked loudly.

I smiled and nodded. "Yes, Roger. I used the books in my classroom the very next day." He looked triumphant, but I felt that I had walked away with the victory.

At face value, this illustration might seem to indicate dishonesty on my part. But I followed the letter of the law in order to avoid an unpleasant and unproductive confrontation with an authority figure who was blatantly trying to use his power to coerce me into doing something I knew I did not have to do.

Ironically, because of our talent at manipulation, we SWCs have a reputation for sometimes being less than honest. In most cases, I believe, the appearance is the result of an SWC's brilliant ability to use circumstances and to achieve goals. Dishonesty itself must be dealt with as sin. It is wrong to lie, and SWCs may lose sight of where the line is drawn. But it is essential that you understand our motivation for doing what we do and realize that your attitude and actions may cause us to resort to circumventing the truth. Again, this does not excuse the SWC from taking responsibility for wrongdoing. We must be accountable for our own actions. Remember, however, that SWCs are usually willing to accept consequences. Not only that, but we may decide that the consequences are worth taking in order to retain our independence and self-control. We cannot and will not let you manipulate and dictate what we do with our lives.

If it's true that the SWC has problems following rules, how do we respond to the concept of a loving God who demands obedience?

DOESN'T GOD DEMAND OBEDIENCE?

During a class I taught for teachers, one of my students, a junior-high teacher, came up to me at the break and asked a question that had been bothering her for some time: "Do you think a strong-willed person can even *be* a Christian?" Before I could reply, she went on to say that she herself was an SWC and had been staying away from church for many years because she felt she wouldn't be able to set aside her individual style and simply conform to the church's many demands.

The answer to her question, of course, is yes. An SWC certainly can be a committed Christian. And it's also true that we have problems following the rules as outlined in many churches. When following God is presented by some to mean following the rules of a particular church or religion, we are suspicious. Who decided what the rules were? How do we know God's Word is being interpreted correctly? To whom are we actually accountable anyway?

Our questions are frequently seen as challenges or insurrections. An SWC who resists going to church with his or her parents may be scolded or even threatened. If an SWC expresses doubts about values or beliefs, he or she may be seen as a rebel. Of course, the more an SWC is reminded to obey the rules and comply with commands, the more the SWC resists and questions. It doesn't take long for the struggle to escalate to mammoth proportions. Relationships can collapse, including that of parent and child and, most important, that of the SWC and God. So what can you do?

Let's look at three situations that must be handled with care in order to avoid a crisis between the SWC and his parents:

1. Your SWC doesn't want to go to church.
Eleven-year-old Kelsey made the announcement calmly at the breakfast table on Sunday morning. "I'm not going to go to church anymore."

Her mother's reaction was swift and disbelieving. "What? You most certainly *are*, young lady. Your father is the *pastor*, for heaven's sake!"

Kelsey's dad looked at her thoughtfully before he spoke. "Kelsey, why don't you want to go to church?"

She shrugged. "I just don't. There's nothing to do. It's boring and I'm tired of it."

"Sometimes I feel that way too." At his daughter's look of surprise, Kelsey's dad continued. "We all get a bit tired of the routine sometimes. But the whole point of going to church is to learn more about God and to spend time with others who want to do the same. Tell me, what do you think would motivate you to want to go to church again?"

"I don't know," she replied.

Her dad scooted his chair closer to her. "Kelsey, what about going to church today and, instead of listening, you write notes about what you think might make things more interesting. There are probably other kids who feel like you do, and you may be able to come up with some great ideas for making church better for *everyone*."

Kelsey was intrigued in spite of herself. "Well," she said, "I think I know some things that would make Sunday a lot more fun."

"Good!" her dad exclaimed. "I'm encouraged already. I think you'll be a great source of ideas for us."

Kelsey stood up and looked around. "Do you know where I could find some paper and a pen?" Her mother was already bringing the necessary supplies.

If your SWC suddenly decides he or she is no longer going to go to church with you, don't react in anger, and don't force the issue. Try to find out why your SWC doesn't want to go, but don't ask impatiently. When you ask why, your SWC may not really know or may not be able to put his feelings into words. Try asking things like "What would motivate you to want to go?" or "What do you think the point of going to church should be?" Make a concerted effort to listen to your SWC's responses. The answers will almost certainly reveal more than you anticipate. Your SWC needs to feel he or she has input. The more you can involve your SWC in coming up with the solution, the better your chances of avoiding the problem in the first place.

2. Your SWC expresses doubts about your church, your beliefs, or your values.

"Everybody cheats a little, Dad."

Max looked at his sixteen-year-old SWC in amazement. "What in the world would make you say a thing like that? You know we do not condone that sort of behavior."

David retorted, "Yeah, well, we don't have much money either."

Max struggled to control his anger. "Son, you know we have always had enough, and we make our money *honestly*."

"But, Dad," David frowned, "it's not like we have to become crooks or anything. It's called *creative financing*."

Max took his son's arm and sat down across the table from him. "Listen, David, I know it's appealing to make a lot of money quickly, even if you have to cheat just a little to do it. I know a lot of people get by with it. But your mother and I have always found that we sleep better knowing we have nothing to hide, no one to fear. It's kept our whole family healthy and happy. If you decide to take a different path, that will be your choice. But check into it carefully. See if the folks you are following down that road are anywhere nearly as happy together as your mom and I are."

David looked exasperated. "Dad, that is so corny."

"I agree. But all I ask is that you check into what you are doing very carefully. I know you want to make money, and I'll help you as much as I can. But I want to do it the old-fashioned way. Let's give it a try my way first, okay?"

David hesitated. "Well, I'm not making any promises. But I'd never expect *you* to cheat."

Max grinned. "That's a start, Son. That's a start."

When your SWC has doubts about what you've believed all your life, meet the issues head-on and face the questions honestly. Your SWC doesn't need for you to provide all the answers, but he does need for you to empathize with his need to find them. Don't make him feel that he's doing something horribly wrong if he expresses doubts about what he believes. Be a guide. Provide the Guide Book, and help your SWC enjoy the journey.

3. Your SWC has turned completely away from God and totally rejects your views.

A friend of mine, Pat, struggled for years with her wayward teenage son. Ray had always been a rebel, and as soon as he graduated from high school, he left home and plunged into the world of sex, drugs, and rock-'n'-roll. Pat and her husband were heartbroken and more than a little discouraged, but they never gave up praying that Ray would change his ways and come home.

I ran into Pat just a few months ago, and her face was absolutely radiant. "Ray's home!" she said happily. "He's a new man! I've got my wonderful boy again." I asked her what changed him, and she smiled. "That's the best part," she declared. "Ray said it wasn't anything we actually told him. He said he just kept remembering all those nights after he went to bed when he heard his dad and me praying for him and thanking God for giving us a son like Ray. He told me it was because we never really preached at him or made him feel like he had to be a certain way in order for us to love him. He said when he felt like he had reached the bottom and had nowhere to go, he remembered what a great place home would be if he could just get there again."

If you have a prodigal son or daughter, you will experience many challenges and moments of pain and sadness. But don't panic and don't judge. Stay calm and loving, and do a lot of praying. In the end your SWC needs to have a safe place to come home to and a reason to return. If he knows he will be assaulted with words of recrimination and reminders of where he went wrong, he will probably do everything he can to avoid you. If, on the other hand, he knows he will always find you praying for him, loving him, and keeping a place open at the table, he will know he has something to come back to. As hard as it is to stay focused, keep asking yourself, "Why would my SWC want to come back?" Make sure your answers are appealing!

IT ALL COMES BACK TO RELATIONSHIPS

When I ask SWCs who are dedicated Christians what motivated them to surrender their lives to God, I get one consistent answer:

We are motivated by the relationship God offers us, not by the punishment we can avoid. In other words, it doesn't work to tell us that unless we surrender to God we will face eternal damnation or hell. In fact, this approach may drive us farther away.

What attracts the SWC to God and to Christianity is the opportunity to be set apart, to be unique. The SWC will often choose not to cross the line between right and wrong. But the SWC must make that decision on his or her own. Sometimes it comes as the result of trying first to succeed without God and finding that it can't be done.

Many parents are justifiably concerned about the eternal well-being of their SWC. It may seem like their child is trying to get as far away from God and the established church as possible. In spite of good intentions, parents may put too much pressure on their SWC to conform to what they know to be true. Unless that SWC finds a way to be valuable and unique in serving a God who is not presented merely as a punitive authority, the parents' best efforts may fail. We SWCs respond better to this good news: God wants each of us to come to Him and to serve Him in a way that enhances the very personality He created within us.

Every SWC needs to know that God is not a narrow, dictatorial authority who offers no choices or alternatives. God does, however, demand obedience. And He certainly has drawn a clear line between right and wrong. In Proverbs 3:5, the Bible states that we should "Trust in the LORD with all your heart, and do not lean on your own understanding" (NASB). I believe that means I don't have the corner on understanding. There may be many approaches, many styles, many ways besides mine. But the very next verse gives me my accountability: "In all your ways acknowledge Him" (NASB). I believe that means that as long as I'm using my style and unique personality to bring honor and glory to God, it's okay. If, on the other hand, I use it in a way that does not acknowledge or bring glory to God, it doesn't matter *what* style I am—it's not okay. That's the bottom line. That's the line that can't be crossed.

I love hearing Steve Green, a contemporary Christian artist, sing one of my favorite songs, "Find Us Faithful." As an SWC whose greatest motivation has always come by way of love and inspiration, I find the words in the chorus especially meaningful:

> May all who come behind us
>
> Find us faithful;
>
> May the fire of our devotion light their way.
>
> May the footprints that we leave
>
> Lead them to believe—
>
> And the lives we lead
>
> *Inspire them to obey.*[1]

There it is in a nutshell:

If you want to motivate me, inspire me.

If you want to direct me, lead the way.

If you want to encourage my ambition, ignite the fire with your enthusiasm.

KEY INSIGHTS FROM THE HEART OF AN SWC

- The quality of your relationship with me determines to a great extent the quality of my relationship with God.
- I am drawn to God because of who He is, not out of the fear of what He could do to me.
- In the end, it will be your love, not your sermons, that keeps me close or brings me back to God and to you.

Be prepared. You're up against far more
than you can handle on your own.
Take all the help you can get, every weapon God has issued,
so that when it's all over but the shouting
you'll still be on your feet.
Truth, righteousness, peace, faith, and salvation
are more than words. Learn how to apply them....
God's Word is an indispensable weapon.
In the same way, prayer is essential in this ongoing warfare.
Pray hard and long.... Keep your eyes open.
Keep each other's spirits up so that no one falls behind or drops out.

Ephesians 6:13-18

CHAPTER EIGHT

When Should I Do Something Drastic?

The telephone rang at 3:02 A.M., according to the digital clock radio. Charles was barely awake, but his wife, Jennifer, was instantly alert. "It's about Angie," she said quietly. Her heart started beating wildly in her chest. Their seventeen-year-old SWC had missed her curfew—again. Somehow Jennifer knew that this transgression would have more serious consequences than others had in the past. Her husband was listening intently to the voice on the telephone and nodding solemnly.

As he hung up, Jennifer was already on her feet. Charles put his head in his hands as he sat on the edge of the bed. He spoke slowly. "Angie was driving. She and Gina and Roger left a wild party, started home by way of Parker Road, and took the corner too fast. The car rolled over several times and hit a tree." Jennifer's face had a look of sheer panic, and Charles continued quickly. "Angie's going to be all right. She was wearing a seat belt and just has a broken arm and some bruises. Roger is in serious condition. Gina didn't make it."

The phone call changed their family life forever. Jennifer and Charles had struggled with Angie's strong-willed nature for years, but during the past twenty-four months their relationship had deteriorated. Angie had made some poor choices when it came to friends, and her schoolwork hit the skids almost immediately. When her parents insisted she improve her grades and control her social life, Angie reacted with extreme rebellion and explosive anger.

Jennifer had sensed their loss of parental control months ago but felt helpless to reverse the situation. Charles just wanted it to go away. Perhaps this was just a phase and they would all grow out of it. But Angie's behavior had continued to spiral downward. Angie shoplifted small items from a corner grocery store. She lied to her mother. She cheated on a test at school and threatened another student. She hung around at parties where kids drank a lot of beer. And Jennifer had recently begun to suspect that Angie was experimenting with drugs as well. Appointments with school counselors, church pastors, and teen-group leaders had all failed to produce any positive results.

And then came the early-morning phone call.

Gina had been Angie's best friend since grade school. When the hospital tested Angie for drugs and alcohol right after the accident, the results showed she was under the influence of both. She was not only in trouble with the law, but she was responsible for the death of the one person she felt understood her. Depression set in swiftly and intensely. Two weeks after the accident, Angie attempted suicide.

Her parents were frantic and, on the advice of a hospital psychologist, had their unwilling daughter committed to a youth rehabilitation center. The center's program was rigorous and unyielding, and Angie's strong will presented a tremendous obstacle to her success there. After she almost succeeded in her second suicide attempt, Angie and her parents met with a highly recommended counselor who specialized in dealing with SWCs. The four of them carefully explored the options and then chose another program that seemed to be more compatible with Angie's style and temperament. Although the road is long and the journey arduous, Angie and her parents are on the upward trail.

Angie's story is not unusual, especially for SWCs. Many of you reading this book have either had a similar experience yourself or have known someone who has been through it. As a result of talking to and working with families like Angie's over the past several years, I have discovered some definite patterns as well as some tried and true strategies for dealing with an SWC who has gone too far. I am not a counselor, and I am certainly not an expert on psychological or criminal behaviors. But I do believe I can share some general guidelines with you that can help you *choose* the right professionals and recognize when you need them most.

HOW WILL YOU KNOW WHEN DEFIANT BEHAVIOR HAS GONE TOO FAR?

Throughout this book, I have given numerous examples of SWC behaviors that do not qualify as defiance or rebellion. I have tried to help you understand why SWCs do many of the things we do. I hope you will be able to repair and nurture the relationships with the SWCs in your life by using those parenting principles and strategies.

But there is a point, difficult as it may be to admit, where parents must admit that their SWC is out of control and their discipline cannot prevent the SWC from harming himself or others.

Here are some questions to help you examine specific areas of your SWC's life and determine whether things have gone too far:

Physical safety: Is your SWC's life in danger? Is your SWC endangering the lives of others?

Moral and spiritual values: Is your SWC deliberately disregarding longstanding household rules or violating your and your family's basic moral values?

Destructive behavior: Is your SWC causing property damage or harming people's possessions, including his or her own?

Dishonesty: Have you caught your SWC deliberately lying or hiding the truth?

If you answered yes to any of the above questions, you should be concerned. If you have lost control over any of these areas, it's time for you to take action.

WHAT TO DO IF YOU'VE LOST CONTROL

If you feel you have lost control over your SWC, it's important to take the following seven decisive steps as quickly as possible.

1. Pray and discuss.

Talk to your spouse or those who support you emotionally. Take an honest look at whether you have lost the ability to control your child. Identify the point at which you lost your ability to influence your SWC. Rededicate your child to God—and commit your desires and efforts to finding and doing God's will.

2. Deal with the issues in front of you.

Try to make your decisions based on what is happening right now. Don't blame others or take on a lot of guilt for past events that led to the current situation. Everyone will certainly share the responsibility. Also, many factors are simply not under your control. Every SWC has a free will, and you can only do so much to influence his or her life choices. Just because you need to call upon professional help doesn't mean you are a failure as a parent. At this point, it will be counterproductive to try to place the blame or to spend your energy criticizing or scolding yourself or others.

3. Decide what you need to accomplish.

The severity of the action you take with your SWC will depend on the nature of your crisis. Although you don't want to overreact, neither do you want to underestimate the seriousness of a potential emotional or substance-abuse problem.

Do you need to separate your SWC from the rest of the family to ensure anyone's physical safety?

Is it likely that your child could attempt suicide?

Does your child simply need time and space for a cooling-off period?

Would it help if the family communicated better?

Decide what your objectives should be for getting help with your SWC. Ideally, you should sit down with the family and make a list of what you feel you need to accomplish. Even if you are dealing with an instantaneous, heat-of-the-moment crisis, take the time to ask that important question: *What's the point? What are we trying to accomplish here?* If you don't know what you want to accomplish, how will you know whether you have been successful?

4. Find the right professionals.

There are effective programs, counselors, and medical/mental-health professionals throughout the nation and the world. But even the most thoroughly professional program with documented success can actually work backwards if it employs techniques that are diametrically opposed to your SWC's nature and mind-set. Knowing this doesn't mean you'll be able to find a program that your SWC will like, but it does mean you'll increase your chances of finding one that actually works over the long haul.

Be sure your professional has documentation of state licenses, memberships in national professional associations, solid credentials, and specific expertise. Beyond that, you can ask some important questions to help determine whether this person or organization will be a good match and work well with your child. Ask:

What is the mission and goal of the organization?

How will you control the behavior of my child?

How will we know the program is successful?

Do you try to break the spirit or simply to control the will? How will you do that?

What kind of training does your staff have that specifically addresses the needs and issues of the strong-willed child?

At what point would we decide the program is or is not going to be successful?

5. *Seek several opinions.*

Don't just grab the first solution that presents itself. Seek the advice of those you trust most, especially those friends or acquaintances who have successfully reared their own SWCs. You will probably get more opinions than you want to hear, and the strongest ones may come from parents who don't have any idea what you are experiencing. Try to keep your perspective and do your best not to let others determine how you feel. Ask more than one health professional about your situation, and press for specialists if you feel it's necessary. Trust your instincts as a parent. Although you don't want to become unreasonable or obsessive, you may have to be assertive with your requests for attention.

Remember, each of these steps will take time. As much as you want to seek immediate relief from a miserable situation, the recovery period for your child may take weeks, months, or even years. Look for and celebrate small victories. Keep your expectations realistic, and stay open to the possibility that you'll need to start over once or twice in order to find the right approach. Don't give up!

6. Don't try to do this by yourself.
Find other parents and family members who understand. Spend your time with those who won't criticize. Do the best you can, and resist the urge to second-guess yourself.

7. Love your SWC, and communicate that love as often as possible.
But don't waver in your resolve to find the best way to keep your

SWC safe and healthy without sacrificing other family members or society in general.

HANG ON TO HOPE

I have never met a parent who wasn't willing to spend any amount of time or money if it meant his or her child would be saved. I have seen dozens of parents who have mortgaged everything they own, who have spent years paying back debts and starting over in new careers just so they could find a way for their SWC to be safe, productive, and successful.

You may be reading this right now through a haze of pain and sorrow because of what your SWC is doing. *While there are no guarantees, there is hope.* The steps you take may have to be unpleasant, expensive, and time-consuming, but *your child is worth it.* God did not give you this child by accident. Trust Him and accept the compliment you have been given. There is help when you have reached the end of your rope. You do not have to go through this alone. This may be the hardest thing you will ever do, but it will most certainly be the most worthwhile.

KEY INSIGHTS FROM THE HEART OF AN SWC

- You may need to rescue me, even when I insist I don't need your help.
- Don't remind me of my failures. Keep emphasizing the progression of my successes.
- Never stop loving me.

God's servant must not be argumentative,
but a gentle listener and a teacher
who keeps cool, working firmly
but patiently with those who refuse to obey.
You never know how or when God might
sober them up with a change of heart
and a turning to the truth.

2 Timothy 2:24-25

CHAPTER NINE

Is It Ever Too Late?

She was in her late fifties, and she was crying as she approached me after one of my seminars for parents of strong-willed children.

"I did everything wrong," she sobbed. "I did and said all those things to my daughter that you just told us won't work." She took a deep breath and began to explain how she had tried to bully her daughter into submission, frequently using threats and severe punishment. "My daughter is grown now," she said sadly, "and she's working as an attorney in California. She returns all of my letters unopened and refuses to communicate with me in any way. How can I even tell her how sorry I am?"

Unfortunately, this mother's plight is like that of dozens of other parents I have spoken to over the years. So many tell me essentially the same thing: "Where were you twenty years ago?" "It's too late now—my strong-willed child is grown." "Why didn't I know this when I could still do something about it?"

IT'S NEVER TOO LATE TO SAY YOU'RE SORRY

The fact is, you *can* do something about it. As long as both you and your SWC are living, it's never too late to begin the process of healing your relationship. For this particular mother, the solution turned out to be simple and straightforward. She mailed a videotape called *Who's Gonna Make Me?* to her daughter with a brief, boldly lettered note on the envelope that read: "Here's what I did wrong—I'm sorry."

She and I agreed there was a good chance her SWC attorney daughter would find it hard to resist the urge to at least take a look at what her mother claimed was an admission of guilt. Once the ice was broken, perhaps they could both talk about the past in less personal terms. I also reminded this mother that she did not have to apologize for the outcomes she had desired— self-discipline, good manners, personal responsibility. She was apologizing for demanding *how* those outcomes be achieved.

Parents of teenage SWCs are often troubled when they realize how different things could have been if they had known more about how the SWC's mind works. Foster Cline and Jim Fay, in their book *Parenting with Love and Logic,* give discouraged parents some reassurance:

> It usually takes one month of love-and-logic parenting to undo one year of tacky parenting. So, if your child is twelve years old, give yourself twelve months to help him or her learn responsible thinking.... It's never too late.... The important thing is to build a relationship with our kids that will last a lifetime—long past the end of the teenage years. And it is never too late to work on that.[1]

I love getting success letters from parents who have made this truth a reality in their families. It's not easy, and they often make several starts and stops before making noticeable progress. But the rewards are incredibly satisfying, and the reclaimed relationship with a son or daughter can last a lifetime. My friend and first professional book editor, Gwen Ellis, recently shared such a letter with me:

> My son and I are very much alike—like a pair of old shoes. There are lots and lots of things we don't need to talk about. We just know what the other is thinking.

That makes it easy for us to be together, have serious discussions, and understand how the other learns.

My daughter and I are very different, and I drive her crazy. I grasp things quickly and am ready to move on to the next thing. She's still back there gathering more and more information before she's ready to move on. You can see how difficult it is for us to communicate. When I began to understand aspects of SWCs and the different learning styles, I began to share what I was reading with her. She began reading your material and learning with me—and what a difference it has made.

We knew we were making progress when the two of us went to a home and garden show. When we came in the door, she stopped me and said, "Mom, I can't stand the way you do these shows. You go here and there and all over the place. How do you know when you've seen everything?" In my mind I thought, *Who cares if you see everything?* I bit my lip because she obviously did care.

"Okay. How do you want to do this?" I asked.

"Let's go around to each booth in a circle."

"All right, but do you have to read every word of every sign?"

"No," she said and grinned.

We proceeded in an orderly fashion around the room and saw what we wanted to see and had an absolutely great time together.

Coming to understand our differences has probably saved our relationship. It taught us that we weren't trying to make each other miserable. We really love each other. What was wrong between us was more about the way we receive and process information than it was about mother-daughter warfare.

My daughter was in her late twenties when we discovered this, and we had been in confrontation for years. But when we both began to learn about each other, we were able to move forward in our relationship and understand we will never approach life in the same way and it's all right. She has also come to understand her brother, who is much like me.

There *is* hope, no matter how long it has been since you and your SWC have had a positive relationship. There won't be any easy answers or quick fixes; genuine, loving, sustained efforts, however, can bring about more changes than you ever thought possible. Frankly, I believe that dealing with an SWC often takes supernatural strength and wisdom. When we try to transform a relationship on our own, we frequently fail. Certainly in my own experience as an SWC child and as the parent of an SWC, a strong faith in God has made all the difference.

HELP! I THINK I'VE BLOWN IT!

If you feel that you've blown it with your SWC, don't give up. I've collected a few tips from my prodigal SWC friends to give you some ideas for bringing your child back. Here are six of them.

1. Start leaving notes.
Point out what you like and appreciate about your child. Thank your SWC for something; give praise for a good idea. Even a quick sticky note on a bedroom door can speak volumes. If your SWC has left home, send notes in a greeting card or with occasional small gifts.

2. Apologize for insisting on always doing things your way.
Explain the outcomes you were trying to achieve and let your SWC know you are open to other suggestions for achieving the same goal.

3. Don't let your SWC scare you away or make you angry.

Hang in there! Let us rant and rave if we must, but remain unmoved when it comes to offering your love. We may tell you there's no hope, we may claim we hate you, we may insist all is lost—*but do not believe it!* We just have to make sure you won't actually give up on us.

4. Be consistent.

We SWCs will watch for a chink in your armor. We'll be suspicious that your new attitude won't last. Try to enlist the help of another family member and identify a code word or phrase. When you are talking to your SWC and that family member hears things beginning to go downhill, he or she can say the code phrase and alert you to what's happening.

5. Find a way to reconnect.

If your SWC has left home, try reestablishing contact by sending a copy of this book to your SWC with a note similar to the one sent by the mother mentioned at the opening of this chapter. By mentioning that the contents may explain what you did wrong, two things might happen: (1) your SWC may be intrigued enough to read it, and (2) your SWC may realize what he or she did wrong as well.

6. Pray.

Many SWCs have told me they were compelled by God to return home, certain the prayers of their family brought them back. While your SWC is at home, pray together whenever possible. Let your child hear you talking to God about your relationship, especially when you're thanking Him for giving you such a great kid. Be specific with God regarding what you like about your SWC. Those prayers can also help remind *you* what you like when the stress level is high!

QUALITIES EVERY PARENT CAN POSSESS

People often ask me how my parents knew what to do with me as I was growing up. How did they know what strategies would work for such a strong-willed child before there were any books about it? Sometimes I even overhear my mom or dad as they answer the questions asked directly to them. They both smile and claim it wasn't as hard as you think. After all, God is good and wise and merciful, and God has always been at the center of their marriage directing their family.

My parents both came from extremely dysfunctional families. My dad—from whom I inherited my strong will, by the way—grew up the son of a wealthy business owner who divorced the mother of his children to marry his secretary. My father and his brother were reared primarily by their mother, who ran a tavern and had many pursuits besides parenting. The two of them learned street smarts right away, and both of them quickly adopted the credo "Only the strong survive."

It was only natural that Dad start drinking at a young age, and his cigarette habit started just as early. Because he and his brother had a great deal of talent, they made a living by playing honky-tonk piano at bars and nightclubs. Their act was "Four Hands on One Piano," and the female clientele especially loved the two handsome men who seemed just as accomplished in wine and women as they did in song.

Dad joined the navy and served in World War II and Korea. He came close to death more than once, and one night, during a drunken stupor in an alley behind a tavern, he stood alone and looked up to the heavens. He was miserable and lonely and fed up with his life. For the first time ever, he prayed: "God, if you're really out there, help me."

Stateside, he rented a tiny room from an elderly lady in Wichita, Kansas. Mrs. Poslick had no formal experience in dealing with strong-willed, rebellious, and wild-living young men. But she did have an extremely strong faith in God, and somehow she knew He wanted this young man to do great things with his life. My dad stayed out late every Saturday night, drinking and partying. Although his Sunday-morning hangovers were acute, Mrs. Poslick's bacon-and-eggs cooking always lured him out of bed. Bleary-eyed and sheepish, he would sit at the breakfast table with this godly woman, and she would feed him until he was full. She didn't flinch when he let the swear words slip out. She didn't lecture him about the strong odors of liquor and cigarettes.

"Bob," she would say pleasantly, after he ate. "Would you like to go to Sunday School with me?" He always groaned to himself. She had been so nice, given him so much. How could he refuse her? Reluctantly, he began to attend church, and God got hold of his life so firmly that a few weeks later he surrendered his heart and his strong will to Christ.

Over the course of the next few months, he decided on his own to quit drinking, smoking, and swearing. He frequently tells the story of how those wonderful church folks never pressured him to give up his vices. He admits he shocked a few of the elderly ladies at first by his language when he testified in church. But they loved him and prayed for him and brought him casseroles and pastries. Not wanting to disappoint them, he cleaned up his act and figured out what was pleasing to his new Lord and Savior. It wasn't long before he knew in his heart that God had called him to be a full-time minister of the gospel that had rescued him in the first place. He accepted the call, used his GI bill to enter a Christian college, and broke the news to his father.

My grandfather had been counting on my dad and uncle to take over the family business. When my dad shared his new faith and calling, my grandfather exploded. Didn't he understand what he was giving up? He was set to make a fortune! This whole Christianity thing was ridiculous! My grandfather said he would take no part in Dad's life if he chose to pursue it. With deep sadness my dad left, praying that somehow God would change his father's heart. Dad enrolled in college and embraced a new life that would eventually include a woman he'd meet there.

My grandfather took quick and decisive action by disowning my father and ostracizing him from the family. Dad spent over forty years praying for his father. He and Dad were personally reconciled a few years later, but it wasn't until a few months before my grandfather died that Dad was given the ultimate gift of leading his strong-willed father to the Lord.

My mom had already finished her college degree when my dad showed up on campus. She worked in the dean's office, and with the help of her boss's matchmaking skills, she met and married my dad. Mom had come from a pretty dysfunctional family herself. Her real mother died giving birth to her, and she was separated from her father and six siblings. She had been adopted by her mother's sister, who raised her in a home where she was welcome but lived uneasily. Her uncle was mentally ill and verbally abusive. She and her aunt both lived in fear of him, and by the time he died (well after my mother had left home), he had inflicted fear and intimidation on both of them.

Despite her upbringing, my mom developed a firm faith in God, and she was determined to make a success of her life. She graduated from college with honors and set a course for a career in business or education. When she married my dad, she was undaunted by his enthusiasm and strong will. Together they began a home mission church in a small town in Missouri, and over the next forty years, their ministry touched thousands of lives.

My dad was an adult before he ever got control of his strong will. There are those who would have said that he seemed, in many ways, beyond redemption. It had gone so far, he had done so much—how could any good come out of this? But one godly woman started praying for him, and loving him, and winning him through her unwavering faith in a God who created the very will that Dad used against Him. Was it too late? Absolutely not! My dad stands as living proof that an errant, strong-willed individual can be redeemed and used for the kingdom of God. My parents reared my sister and me in a home that bore no resemblance to the dysfunctional ones they came from. We were grounded in faith, dedicated to service, and educated in the ways of both heaven and the world.

When I asked my dad to write a paragraph or two from his point of view for this chapter, he penned the following note to me:

You knew that your mom and I loved each other deeply, and that you never had to worry about our commitment to Jesus and to each other. Remember the story you told about us holding hands under the breakfast table? We are still doing it.

We never brought home the personal problems of those we ministered to. No matter what anyone did, Mom and I never became bitter or negative, and we were never any different at home than we were in public.

It was in Reno that we decided there was power in positive thinking, and challenged you and Sandee to look at life in a positive rather than in a negative way. Remember it cost us a nickel a negative word? That didn't last long, because we couldn't afford it!

You have stated the facts clearly and concisely in a beautiful way. You are still directing a strong will

sanctified by Jesus in a loving, generous, positive way.
Thank you for making your mother and me a great
part of your life—even up to this very minute.

It's true my parents had no formal training in raising a spir-
ited and strong-willed child like me. But they did have two things
that every parent can possess—a life wholly and firmly committed to God and an unconditional love for their strong-willed child.
In the end, these qualities are what really matters.

KEY INSIGHTS FROM THE HEART OF AN SWC

- I will never be too old to appreciate hearing what you
  like about me.
- I am never completely beyond your reach. Sometimes
  I just need an excuse to take your hand.
- You don't have to be an expert on strong wills to
  show your consistent love for me.

*Go easy on those
who hesitate in the faith.
Go after those who take the wrong way.
Be tender with sinners,
but not soft on sin.*

Jude 22-23

A Last Word

Remember,

You Can't Make Me.

So don't:

- back me into a corner and leave me no choice,
- tell me what I will or will not do,
- insist that something can't be done,
- demand I obey without question.

But I Can Be Persuaded!

So do:

- value my ability to see the world from a unique perspective,
- find ways to inspire me to change the world,
- ask me for my input,
- recognize my uniqueness even if it bothers you.

Your strong-willed child will keep you forever challenged. You won't have to worry about becoming bored or getting into a rut. There's a lot to be said for that! I hope this book has given you a glimpse into the minds and hearts of SWCs, and I especially hope you can keep a different perspective in your relationships with all of the SWCs in your life. Life is too short to constantly battle those you love. If you can begin to understand the inner workings of an SWC's mind, you may hold the key to his or her heart. It sure beats knocking down the door!

If you have benefited from this book, I'd love to hear from you. Perhaps you have a success story that would help others; maybe you have unanswered questions I could address in a future book. Please drop me a line, and I'll do my best to address your issues and concerns. You can contact me at:

AppLe St. (Applied Learning Styles)
P.O. Box 1450
Sumner, WA 98390

Blessings to you and all your SWCs!

Notes

Chapter 1:   Who Is the Strong-Willed Child?

1. James Dobson, *The Strong-Willed Child* (Wheaton, Ill.: Tyndale, 1978), 15. Used by permission. All rights reserved.
2. Dobson, *The Strong-Willed Child*, 10.
3. Franklin Graham, *Rebel with a Cause* (Nashville: Nelson, 1995), 10-1.

Chapter 2:   How Do I Build a Positive Relationship with My Strong-Willed Child?

1. Cynthia Ulrich Tobias, *Every Child Can Succeed* (Colorado Springs, Colo.: Focus on the Family, 1996), Preface.

Chapter 3:   How Do I Motivate My Strong-Willed Child?

1. Dobson, *The Strong-Willed Child*, 99.

Chapter 4:   So What's the Big Deal About School?

1. Foster Cline, M.D., and Jim Fay, *Parenting with Love and Logic* (Colorado Springs, Colo.: Piñon Press, 1990), 28,51. Used by permission of Piñon Press Publishing. All rights reserved. For copies of the book, call 800-366-7788.

2. Send a self-addressed, stamped envelope and a request for a student profile to AppLe St., P.O. Box 1450, Sumner, WA 98390.

3. See Peter R. Breggin and Ginger Ross Breggin, *The War Against Children: How the Drugs, Programs, and Theories of the Psychiatric Establishment Are Threatening America's Children with a Medical "Cure" for Violence* (New York: St. Martin's Press, 1994), 110.

4. Thomas Armstrong, *The Myth of the A.D.D. Child: 50 Ways to Improve Your Child's Behavior and Attention Span Without Drugs, Labels, or Coercion* (New York: Dutton Books, 1995).

5. Robert Martin, *Teaching through Encouragement* (Englewood Cliffs, N.J.: Prentice-Hall, 1980), 7.

6. Breggin and Breggin, *The War Against Children*, 110.

Chapter 5:   How Can I Best Discipline My Strong-Willed Child?

1. Cline and Fay, *Parenting with Love and Logic*, 61.

2. Dobson, *The Strong-Willed Child*, 100.

3. Cline and Fay, *Parenting with Love and Logic*, 72.

Chapter 7:   What About the Line Between Right and Wrong?

1. "Find Us Faithful," words and music by Jon Mohr.
Copyright © 1987 Jonathan Mark Music and
Birdwing Music. All rights controlled by Gaither
Copyright Management. Used by permission.

Chapter 9:   Is It Ever Too Late?

1. Cline and Fay, *Parenting with Love and Logic*, 103.

Recommended Resources

Armstrong, Thomas. *The Myth of the A.D.D. Child: 50 Ways to Improve Your Child's Behavior and Attention Span Without Drugs, Labels, or Coercion.* New York: Dutton Books, 1995.

A former special-education teacher, Dr. Armstrong provides fifty practical, positive ways to help that child who has been labeled A.D.D. (attention deficit disorder). His heartfelt and well-researched position is that A.D.D. does not exist; that the children who experience behavioral and attention-related problems are healthy human beings with a unique style of thinking and learning.

Breggin, Peter R., and Ginger Ross Breggin. *The War Against Children: How the Drugs, Programs, and Theories of the Psychiatric Establishment Are Threatening America's Children with a Medical "Cure" for Violence.* New York: St. Martin's Press, 1994.

Dr. Peter Breggin is a psychiatrist who has taken a stand against the use of medication for social control of children and their behaviors. He and his wife have written this compelling book, providing a host of alternative measures for fulfilling the genuine and often inconvenient needs of children.

Chess, Stella, and Alexander Thomas. *Know Your Child: An Authoritarian Guide for Today's Parents.* New York: Basic Books, 1987.

This volume is packed with evidence (including longitudinal research studies) that each child has his own unique temperament from the beginning to the end of his life. Their "goodness of fit" theory has practical applications for successful parenting.

Cline, M.D., Foster, and Jim Fay. *Parenting Teens with Love and Logic: Preparing Adolescents for Responsible Adulthood.* Colorado Springs: Piñon Press, 1993.

Whether you've used the love-and-logic approach all along or are looking for some extra help during adolescence, this book will give you a fresh look at discipline, self-esteem, and common struggles parents have with their teenagers. You win because you'll learn to love and effectively guide your teens without resorting to anger, threats, or power struggles. Your teens win because they'll learn responsibility and problem solving with the tools they'll need to cope in the real world.

Cline, M.D., Foster, and Jim Fay. *Parenting with Love and Logic: Teaching Children Responsibility.* Colorado Springs: Piñon Press, 1990.

If you want to raise kids who are self-confident, motivated, and ready for the real world, take advantage of this win-win approach to parenting. The information in this book can not only revolutionize your relationships with your children, but it might also put the fun back into parenting!

Fay, Jim, and David Funk. *Teaching with Love and Logic: Taking Control of the Classroom.* Golden, Colo.: Love and Logic Press, 1995.

This book will give you practical solutions to the day-to-day frustrations and challenges common in today's classroom. Following these tried-and-true techniques can reduce the time and energy you spend maintaining discipline in the classroom, and let you put some fun back into teaching.

Glenn, H. Stephen, and Jane Nelsen. *Raising Self-Reliant Children in a Self-Indulgent World: Seven Building Blocks for Developing Capable Young People.* Rocklin, Calif.: Prima Publishing, 1989.

A wonderful, practical, and real-world handbook for helping even strong-willed children learn to be independent without getting away with bad behavior. You'll love the evenhanded, down-to-earth approach authored by these two parents, one a parent of seven, the other a parent of four and foster parent of twenty.

Graham, Franklin. *Rebel with a Cause: Finally Comfortable Being a Graham.* Nashville: Thomas Nelson, 1995.

A great story of a strong-willed prodigal son who came home. You'll read some amazing accounts of classic strong-willed behavior, and you'll know that if Franklin Graham can come home, there will always be hope for your own prodigal!

Gregorc, Anthony F. *An Adult's Guide to Style*, Columbia, Conn.: Gregorc Associates, 1982.

The definitive volume for identifying and understanding Gregorc's model of learning styles. Packed with definitions and examples, you'll find this book an essential reference for serious study.

Keirsey, David, and Marilyn Bates. *Please Understand Me: Character and Temperament Types.* Del Mar, Calif.: Prometheus, Nemesis, 1978.

This book provides a fascinating look at personality types and temperaments. You'll discover how your temperament affects your success in relationships, careers, and life in general.

Spears, Dr. Dana Scott, and Dr. Ron L. Braund. *Strong-Willed Child or Dreamer? Understanding the Crucial Differences Between a Strong-Willed Child and a Creative-Sensitive Child.* Nashville: Thomas Nelson, 1996.

Two leading child-and-family counselors share valuable insights and practical strategies for helping parents understand children who are driving them crazy. You'll find yourself nodding your head throughout the book as you read about yourself and identify the strengths of your children.

Tobias, Cynthia Ulrich. *Every Child Can Succeed: Making the Most of Your Child's Learning Style.* Colorado Springs: Focus on the Family, 1995.

This book is filled with practical ideas for applying learning styles to motivation, discipline, and much more. Copyright-free profiles contained in the appendix can help parents and children record and summarize learning-style strengths for their teachers.

Tobias, Cynthia Ulrich, with Paul Tomlinson. *Putting Your Style to Work: Practical Strategies for Using Your Learning Style Strengths on the Job.* Seattle: AppLe St., 1996.

Three audiotapes plus a workbook and Delineator. Practical and entertaining discussion about strategies for discovering and making the most of learning-style strengths in the workplace, even when one's strengths are at odds with another's strengths in the same office. Talks about finding your niche, dealing with a difficult boss or employee, and bringing out the best in your teammates.

Tobias, Cynthia Ulrich. *The Way They Learn: How to Discover and Teach to Your Child's Strengths.* Colorado Springs: Focus on the Family, 1994.

An international bestseller, this entertaining and practical book should be required reading for any parent or teacher who truly wants to help his children succeed. These concepts are powerful tools for bringing out the best in every child.

Tobias, Cynthia Ulrich. *The Way We Work: A Practical Approach for Dealing with People on the Job.* Nashville: Broadman & Holman, 1999.

An enlightening and easy-to-read resource for developing more efficient communication with those with whom you work. This is a powerful plan for transforming your on-the-job relationships!

Tobias, Cynthia Ulrich, with Nick Walker. *"Who's Gonna Make Me?" Effective Strategies for Dealing with the Strong-Willed Child.* Seattle: Chuck Snyder & Associates, 1992.

Focusing on the Concrete Random strong-willed child, this forty-five-minute video presents practical, hands-on strategies for bringing out the best in your strong-willed child.

About the Author

Cynthia Ulrich Tobias is founder, manager, and CEO of AppLe St. (Applied Learning Styles) and president of Learning Styles Unlimited, Inc. In addition to a busy speaking schedule, Cynthia coordinates the AppLe St. education and commerce programs and administers various learning-styles projects throughout North America and in several foreign countries.

A best-selling author, Cynthia is a popular speaker at workshops, classes, and seminars for businesses, government agencies, churches, and school districts. She earned her bachelor of arts in education from Northwest Nazarene College and her master of education degree from Seattle Pacific University.

Cynthia lives with her husband, John, and their twin boys in the Seattle, Washington, area.

About AppLe St.

AppLe St. is an international organization dedicated to helping people identify, value, and utilize their individual strengths. The organization offers encouragement, affirmation, and a fundamental framework for understanding and applying *learning styles*—the ways in which people perceive and process information—to the process of education.

The educational division of AppLe St. provides in-service training, curricular and learning-styles assessments, and training for teachers in public, private, and home-school settings. The corporate division offers consulting services and seminar facilitators to businesses.

For more information contact:

AppLe St.

P.O. Box 1450

Sumner, WA 98390

(253) 862-6200

website: www.applest.com